CHOCOLATE

Love, Lexi

LETTERS TO GOD

BY SHERRY KYLE

Tyndale House Publishers, Inc.
Carol Stream, Illinois

Visit Tyndale online at www.tyndale.com.

Visit Sherry Kyle online at www.sherrykyle.com.

TYNDALE and Tyndale's quill logo are registered trademarks of Tyndale House Publishers, Inc.

Love, Lexi: Letters to God

Designed by Jacqueline L. Nuñez

Edited by Sarah Rubio

Published in association with Books & Such Literary Management, Rachel Kent, 52 Mission Circle, Suite 122, PMB 170, Santa Rosa, CA 95409-5370.

Scripture quotations are taken from the *Holy Bible*, New Living Translation, copyright © 1996, 2004, 2015 by Tyndale House Foundation. Used by permission of Tyndale House Publishers, Inc., Carol Stream, Illinois 60188. All rights reserved.

For manufacturing information regarding this product, please call 1-800-323-9400.

ISBN 978-1-4964-0963-8

Printed in the United States of America

22	21	20	19	18	17	16
7	6	5	4	3	2	1

To girls who feel stuck in the middle

CHOCOLATE

Hi, God,

I'll get straight to the point. Today was the WORST DAY EVER!

I got in trouble this morning when Mom saw my messy room. I forgot to pick up my dirty clothes from the floor, and it literally looked like a bomb went off. Mom yelled, "Alexis Dawn Cooper, if you don't clean up your room this minute, you'll be grounded for a month!" Those were her exact words.

Then at school my friend Ellie practically told Justin that I had a crush on him! Can you believe it???

What made it worse was that Bianca found out. GRRR!!! Now she has more information she can use to embarrass me in front of the entire school. What can I say? Bianca doesn't call me "Lexi the Loser" for nothing. Ellie and Abby have been my only two friends since kindergarten.

So here's what happened, according to Abby.

Ellie handed Justin a note at recess that said,

Do you like Lexi Cooper?

___ Yes

___ No

1

Of course, Bianca was standing by our locker when Justin handed the note back to Ellie. She waited until he walked away, then she whipped the note from Ellie's hand.

When I showed up, Bianca tossed the note at me and said, "Too bad. Justin must like blondes better." She flipped her long, blonde hair over her shoulder and strutted away.

I looked at the note . . . and about had a heart attack!

The good part is that Justin checked YES! The bad part is that he wrote "as a friend" next to it.

As I watched Bianca go down the hall, I thought about all kinds of mean things I wanted to do to her, like pull her perfectly shiny hair or call her something like "Queen Wanna Bee," but instead I just stood there.

Abby leaned over and whispered, "Bianca thinks she can say whatever she wants because she's the PD." (That's our code for "principal's daughter.")

That may be true, but it didn't make me feel better.

Then Ellie said, "Don't worry, there are TONS of other guys in middle school."

All I know is that I've liked Justin since first grade when he shared his peanut butter and jelly sandwich with me. He even gave me one of his chocolate chip cookies. YUM!

But back to today . . .

During English class, Mrs. Anderson paired us off. We were supposed to write a short story about a real-life experience and read it to our partner. Guess who the teacher paired me up with? Yep, BIANCA TAYLOR!

I wrote about when I saved my little brother from having to visit the ER when he stuck a LEGO up his nose.

Thank goodness I was able to get it out using my mom's eyebrow tweezers.

When it was time to read our stories, Bianca wanted to go first. She had written about the time when she was the princess in the school play and Justin was the prince. She went on and on about how they were the perfect royal couple. GAG!

Just because I have a major crush on Justin doesn't mean she has to like him too. Cuz when it comes right down to it, I know he'd pick Bianca over me any day.

Here's why:

(I know I shouldn't compare, but I just can't help myself.)

Me	Bianca
Brown, frizzy hair	Perfect, blonde, straight hair
Short	Medium height
Freckles with a few zits	Flawless, clear skin
No talent whatsoever	Can sing and dance

See? I don't have a chance.

Except Justin did say he was my friend, and that's better than nothing and more important, anyway.

Yeah, right!

I've been avoiding Justin all day. I can't face him! And I don't know if I'll be able to all year.

Bianca, on the other hand, can stay as far away from me as possible.

Maybe I am a loser with a capital L.

Thank goodness You love me. Right?

Love, Lexi ♡

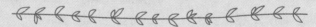

Dear Lexi,

Nothing can separate you from My love—not death or life, not angels or demons, not your fears for today or your worries about tomorrow, not even the powers of hell. Not any power in the sky or on the earth or anywhere else in all creation. I love you with an ever-lasting love. (Romans 8:38-39; Jeremiah 31:3)

Love, God

One-of-a-Kind You!

When you compare yourself with others, it's easy to feel like you don't measure up. You'll always be able to find someone who you feel is better than you in some area. But God created you special and one-of-a-kind, and He loves you *just the way you are*—with your unique looks, talents, and personality. That's right, He likes your hair that way! He loves the shape of your nose, the color of your skin, and the sound of your laugh. You are made in God's image, and you are exactly how He designed you to be.

What's YOUR Story?

Hi, God,

Sometimes I feel like a loser. Here's why:

_____

_____

_____

_____

_____

_____

_____

_____

_____

_____

_____

_____

_____

_____

But when I think about how much YOU love me, I feel . . .

_____

_____

_____

_____

_____

_____

_____

_____

_____

_____

_____

_____

Thank you for making me just the way I am. Help me not to compare myself with others.

Love, _____

*May you have the power to understand, as
all God's people should, how wide, how long,
how high, and how deep his love is.*
Ephesians 3:18

 CHOCOLATE

Friday, September 2

Dear God,

I love chocolate. I love chocolate milk, chocolate cake, and chocolate candy bars. I love chocolate ice cream, chocolate chip cookies, and chocolate cream pie. I love, love, love chocolate!!!

So when Mr. Kramer, my history teacher, passed out a packet in homeroom to sell cookie dough and chocolate to raise money for the new computer lab, I was in heaven. I have $16.82 in my piggy bank, and I know exactly how I'm going to spend it. On chocolate!

On the way home from school, Ellie and I sat as close as we dared to the cool kids in the back of the bus. We'd barely pulled out of the parking lot when Ellie said, "I'm going to start selling as soon as I get home. What about you?"

I told her the ONLY way my mom will let me sell is if Kate goes with me. When will Mom realize I'm not a baby anymore?

"Your sister is so nice. I'm sure she'll help you out," Ellie said.

I almost fell out of my seat!

Kate never does anything with me unless my mom promises to let her hang out with her friends, go shopping, or watch her favorite television show. Basically, Kate thinks I'm an annoying little sister who gets into all her stuff. Okay, I admit I tried on her perfume and looked through her magazine, but I couldn't help myself.

I saw an article about how to get rid of zits, and I just had to read it. If only I'd remembered to put the magazine back on the shelf and the cap back on her perfume!

Well, you would've thought I committed the worst possible crime if you'd heard the way Kate went on and on about her private property. It wasn't like I stole anything. I thought she was going to draw a line down the center of our room—or kick me out and make me sleep in our little brother's room!

Ellie laughed when I told her the story. "Only you would forget to get rid of the evidence. Does this have anything to do with YOU KNOW WHO?" She wiggled her brows and turned toward where Justin sat a couple of rows back. I tugged on her arm and told her to stop looking.

If only my face was perfect like Bianca's. I hate to admit how jealous I am of her clear skin. Speaking of Bianca, she's been hanging around Justin more than usual. I can't compete with her natural beauty.

But back to cookie dough and chocolate . . .

We have only four weeks to sell it. Mr. Kramer said the deadline to hand in the orders is September 30, and the grand prize is a limousine ride and a pizza lunch with up to three friends at Pizza My Heart. Ellie, Abby, or I need to sell the most and win!

Before Ellie got off the bus, she made me promise to ask Kate to sell with me.

Once the door closed, I slunk down in my seat, brainstorming how I could convince my sister, when a boy behind

me said, "Why should I raise money for the school? I have my own computer at home. We'll be out of middle school in a couple of years. It's not worth it."

Another boy chimed in. "Yeah, selling candy is a lot of work. I'll sell to my grandma, but other than that, I'm not going to bother."

The competition was getting smaller by the minute. I grinned, but my smile faded when I recognized Bianca's screechy voice. "I'm going to win because my father is the principal of Green Acres Middle School and knows EVERYONE in town."

Why does Bianca ride the bus, anyway? Couldn't she go home with her dad? It would make my life a lot easier.

Bianca continued. "Did you see the grand prize? A limousine ride and a pizza party. Have you ever ridden in a limo?" Bianca was looking right at Justin, MY Justin.

"No," he said, "but I'd like to one day. A few months ago my aunt got married, and they rode away in a limo. Looked pretty cool."

"Perfect," Bianca squealed. "If I win the grand prize, you are coming with me."

"O-kay . . ." Justin didn't sound too sure of himself, which gave me a tiny bit of satisfaction.

"It's official," Bianca purred. "We have a date!"

Several other boys asked if they could go too, but Bianca said no. Before she got off the bus, she gave me a smug grin.

That girl makes me SO MAD!!! As much as I want to win, I want Bianca to lose even more. There is NO WAY I'm going to allow her to spend time alone with MY crush—even if I have to promise to do Kate's chores for a month!

God, is it okay to . . . seriously dislike someone? I would say "hate," but I always get in trouble when I use that word.

Love, Lexi ♡

Dear Lexi,
I say, love your enemies! Pray for those who persecute you! (Matthew 5:44)
Love, God

Love Your Enemies

Enemies are people who hurt you with what they do and say, and they can make your life miserable if you allow it. God says you are to love your enemies and pray for them. When you do this, you might see a difference in how they treat you. But even if they don't change their actions, your attitude toward your enemies will change. You will find yourself looking at them through God's eyes. And you will feel His peace as you allow Him to heal your hurt.

What's YOUR Story?

Dear God,

I have an enemy. Here's what's happening:

_____

_____

_____

_____

_____

_____

_____

_____

_____

_____

_____

_____

_____

_____

_____

_____

_____

_____

_____

_____

_____

_____

12

With your help I can show kindness to my enemy by . . .

_____

_____

_____

_____

_____

_____

_____

_____

_____

_____

_____

_____

_____

_____

_____

_____

_____

_____

_____

Thank you for healing my hurts. Help me to love my enemies, even when it's hard.

Love, _____

The whole law can be summed up in this one command: "Love your neighbor as yourself."

Galatians 5:14

Monday, September 5

Dear God,

Kate was hardly home all weekend, so by this afternoon I still hadn't sold any chocolate or cookie dough. Why does Kate have to be a cheerleader when I need her? I stomped my foot on the tile floor in the kitchen, then realized I'd better tone it down or else Mom might suspect something.

Too late!

"Okay, spill." Mom threw me That Look. Her right eyebrow inched upward, and her mouth puckered. "What's going on?"

I couldn't tell Mom that unless I sold the most chocolate and cookie dough, Justin would be riding in a limo and eating pizza with Bianca. Instead I told her about the fund-raiser and how important it was for the school to raise money for new computers.

That's when my day took a DRASTIC turn!

Ben raced into the kitchen wearing his blanket tied around his neck like a cape.

"Slow down!" Mom called. She tried to trap him, but he was too quick.

He dodged her and ran around the room, laughing. "You can't catch me."

"Ben, I mean it. Slow down before you hurt yourself." Mom opened the dishwasher as Ben tore around the corner.

Ben made a quick move to the left, his socks gliding

over the slippery tile like a skater on ice. His right leg went one way and his left flew the other. Then he landed with a crack and a loud thud against the corner of the cabinet.

"Oh, my head." Ben grabbed the back of his skull. Blood oozed out and trickled down his neck.

My stomach flipped over, and the room started to spin. "He's bleeding!"

Mom grabbed a dish towel and held it against the back of Ben's head. "Alexis, sit down before you faint." She let out a breath. "I can't handle two kids needing stitches."

I folded myself cross-legged onto the cold tile floor.

Tears slid down Ben's face. "I don't want stitches!"

"Let me take a look." Mom pulled the towel away and peeked. "I think you need them, buddy. It looks pretty deep."

Ben cried louder.

When I looked at the red-stained towel, my stomach felt like it was going to explode!

Mom pointed toward the family room. "Lexi, grab your brother's shoes. We need to see Doctor Fischer." She wrapped an arm around Ben's waist and helped him stand while keeping the towel against his head.

I gulped and ran to the front door, where I found Ben's shoes, the shoelaces tied up in knots. I grabbed them and hurried to the garage, where Mom was helping Ben into the car.

Mom's eyes bored into mine. "You hold the towel while I drive."

Was she kidding? Mom knows the sight of blood makes

me queasy. My mouth went dry. "But what about the fund-raiser? Can't I sell door-to-door while you're at the doctor's office with Ben?"

Mom tossed her purse in the passenger seat. "Lexi, please just get in the car and buckle up."

I wanted to argue that Ben could hold the towel by himself. But he looked so sad with his mouth drooping and his cheeks stained with tears. I clicked my seat belt, sucked in a breath, and reached over to hold the towel in place over Ben's gash. I just wouldn't look.

On the drive, I tried to keep my mind busy. I looked at the buildings and trees lining the streets and wished I lived closer to Ellie and Abby. An idea formed, but I decided to keep it to myself until AFTER the doctor stitched up my brother.

I sat in the waiting room while Ben and Mom saw the doctor. The minutes ticked by slowly. It seemed to take HOURS, but after glancing at the clock I realized they were done in twenty minutes.

"How many stitches did you get?" I laid a hand on Ben's shoulder.

He wiggled his fingers. "Five, cuz I'm five years old." He chose a sticker and stuck it on his shirt.

"Cool." I smiled. "You're one brave kid."

Mom led us out of the doctor's office to the parking lot. Now was as good a time as any to bring up my idea. "So, Mom—"

"I need to go to the grocery store before I pick up Kate from cheerleading practice." Mom pressed the remote button attached to her keys and unlocked the car doors. "But I'll take you two home first."

Ben and I piled into the car.

"But I want to go too." Ben rubbed his eyes.

"After the fall you had, I think it's best if you rest this afternoon. I'll be back as soon as I can."

On the ride home, I folded my arms tight across my chest. It seems like the world revolves around Kate and Ben. When did Mom and Dad ever drop everything for me? I tried to conjure up a memory, but nothing came to mind.

Time to tell Mom my idea.

"Hey, Mom, can Ellie and Abby come over tomorrow after school? I thought we could take turns selling chocolate and cookie dough in each other's neighborhoods. Like you always say, 'Safety in numbers.'"

"I'll have to check my calendar," Mom said.

If I could count the times Mom has said those exact words, it would be close to a BAJILLION by now. I had a sneaking suspicion that if there were anything written down for tomorrow it would have Kate's or Ben's name on it. I sank lower in my seat, my attitude going down with me.

Once we were home, I shut the garage door as Mom pulled away. I walked into the kitchen and stared at the corner of the cabinet where Ben had whacked his head. I noticed a drop of blood along with a few strands of his hair wedged into the splintered wood. Poor kid. He hit it hard.

TV sounds came from the family room where Ben was snuggled under his blanket on the couch, watching his favorite cartoon. He'd probably stay there the whole time Mom was gone.

I unzipped my backpack and pulled out the fund-raising packet. Maybe I could start by calling all my parents' friends. Better yet, I could e-mail them. I'm not allowed to use the Internet when Mom and Dad aren't home, but I was sure they would understand and make an exception this once. Right?

Love, Lexi

Dear Lexi,
Honor your father and mother. Then you will live a long, full life in the land I give you. (Exodus 20:12)
Love, God

⑧bey Your Parents

God created families and gave parents authority to help their children make good decisions. You may not understand why your parents make certain rules or why you have to do what they tell you, like clean your room or wash the dishes, but it's important to obey in order to learn responsibility, the difference between right and wrong, and how to treat other people. Most importantly, when you obey your parents, you are pleasing God.

What's YOUR Story?

Dear God,

I'm facing a choice to either obey or disobey my parents. Here's what's happening:

_____

_____

_____

_____

_____

_____

_____

_____

_____

_____

_____

_____

_____

_____

_____

_____

_____

_____

_____

20

I can choose to obey them by . . .

_____

_____

_____

_____

_____

_____

_____

_____

_____

_____

_____

_____

_____

_____

_____

Thank you for my parents. Help me to honor them by doing what they say.

Love, _____

Children, always obey your parents,
for this pleases the Lord.
Colossians 3:20

Dear God,

I was so WRONG!

Mom was really upset when she found out I used the computer while she wasn't home. She said, "Alexis Dawn Cooper, you know the rules!" Then she grounded me from the computer for the rest of the month. AAARGH! No computer games for 25 more days. And no messaging or e-mail.

Kate was sprawled on her bed doing homework and smacking her gum like a cow chewing its cud. (I read that in a book once. Pretty disgusting!) When she heard me complain about my life being totally ruined, she said, "You can always call people."

Now, why didn't I think of using my cell phone? BECAUSE I DON'T HAVE ONE!

Hopefully I'm not banned from using the house phone too. I stopped pacing and stared at my sister.

I must've stared too long, because she turned her head in my direction and said in her nasty sister voice, "What's the matter with you?"

I shrugged a shoulder and flopped back on my bed, trying to ignore how much her words hurt. That's when I saw a spider on the ceiling. I screamed and pointed to the eight-legged monster making its way toward MY side of the room.

"You're such a baby." Kate emptied her pencil jar, grabbed a dirty sock off the floor, and stood on her desk. With a flick of her wrist, she pushed the spider into the container. "Sure you don't want Mr. Spider on your bed?" She held the jar over my head.

Thank goodness for Ben!

Yes, he annoys me by always pretending to be someone he's not—like a superhero or a dinosaur—but when he walked into the bedroom and begged me to read him a book, I jumped up at the chance and raced to his room. Kate's laughter floated down the hall.

Sisters can be SO MEAN!

After I read Ben a good-night story, I lay beside him, thinking about how I was going to approach Mom and Dad about using the phone. I stayed there until Ben fell asleep and I heard the garage door open, which wasn't the best idea since I hadn't finished my homework yet.

The way I saw it, I had two options:

Tell Mom and Dad the truth (which in my experience always ends up being the best answer)

OR

Fib a little

When I heard footsteps on the stairs, I hoped it was Dad. According to Mom, he can be too lenient. All I know is that he sometimes lets me get away with stuff, especially after a busy day at work.

The minute Mom walked in, I blurted, "There's a spider in our room, and Kate's going to put it on my bed!"

Mom kissed the top of Ben's head, pulled the covers higher under his chin, and escorted me out of the room. "Poor baby," she said. "It's been a rough few days."

At first I thought Mom meant ME, but when I repeated her words in my head, I realized she was talking about Ben.

"Did you hear what I said?" I stood on tiptoes, trying to get Mom's attention. (I hate being short.) "Kate was going to put a SPIDER on my bed!"

Mom covered a laugh. "Have you been hiding out in Ben's room all night?"

I didn't see what was so funny, but it did give me a real reason for not having my homework done.

On the way to my bedroom, I confessed that I still needed to do my math. Mom didn't seem to mind. "Okay, but hurry up."

What bugged me was that Kate never got in trouble. Mom told her not to tease me, but I expected her to be grounded like I was for the next few weeks. I know for some people, spiders are no big deal, but I hyperventilate if one gets too close. Honestly, I think Kate just wanted the room to herself.

I used to like being a middle child, and it does kind of have its perks. For one, I never get lonely. I'm either hanging out with Kate in our room or playing a game with Ben (when he begs). I always thought it was a good thing to have siblings, but lately I've changed my mind. Now I wonder what it's like to be an only child, like Bianca. I bet she always gets her way!

The second thing I like about being in the middle is that my parents don't expect as much from me as they do

23

from Kate, and they don't make me go to bed as early as Ben. But lately, I feel invisible.

Do you see me, God? Do you care that I'm afraid of spiders and can't stand the sight of blood?

Love, Lexi 🤍

> *Dear Lexi,*
> *The very hairs on your head are all numbered. So don't be afraid; you are more valuable to Me than a whole flock of sparrows. (Matthew 10:30-31)*
> *Love, God*

You Are Valuable

God knows everything about you, including your favorite color, your fears, what you think about, and what makes you smile. He even knows how many freckles you have. In fact, the Bible says He saw you before you were born. You are never invisible to God!

What's YOUR Story?

Dear God,

I feel invisible. Here's why:

_____

_____

_____

_____

_____

_____

_____

_____

_____

_____

_____

_____

_____

_____

_____

_____

_____

_____

_____

26

I know you see me because . . .

_____

_____

_____

_____

_____

_____

_____

_____

_____

_____

_____

_____

_____

_____

_____

_____

_____

_____

_____

_____

Thank you for knowing everything about me! Help me to conquer my fears.

Love, _____

CHOCOLATE

You saw me before I was born.
Every day of my life was recorded in your book.
Psalm 139:16

Wednesday, September 7

Dear God,

You'll never guess what happened to me today. I had the most WONDERFUL and CONFUSING moments of my entire life!

Here's what happened. (I can tell it's going to be a L-O-N-G letter!)

"Why weren't you on the bus this morning?" Ellie asked the minute I stepped out of Mom's car.

"My brother spilled his milk, and it took my mom and me forever to mop it up. By the time I got to the bus stop, the bus was long gone."

We walked into the school and stood by our locker.

I glanced over my shoulder. "Where's Abby?"

"Not here yet." Ellie flipped her braid over her shoulder. "Did you hear about her dad?"

I shook my head. "What about him?"

"Abby said he might take a job in New York."

My stomach twisted into a knot. "What? She's moving?"

"I'm not sure, but Abby was pretty upset last night," Ellie said. "How come you didn't answer our messages?"

Figures I'd get in trouble right before one of my best friends needed me. "I'm grounded from the computer."

Ellie leaned in. "What'd you do this time?"

"I used the computer while my mom was out." I fidgeted with the strap of my backpack. "Hey, Kate wasn't home, and I wanted to start selling chocolate and cookie dough.

I e-mailed a bunch of my parents' friends to see if they wanted to buy some."

"Good idea," Ellie said. "Did you sell any?"

"I sold three boxes of chocolate. How about you?"

"I went around my neighborhood and sold one box of chocolate and five tubs of cookie dough. Not much, but my dad took the catalog to work today."

"Good idea."

The school bell rang.

I tugged on Ellie's arm. "Let's hurry, before we're late to class."

We scrambled down the hall to first period and nearly ran into Justin when we rounded the corner. I felt heat rush up my neck and settle in my cheeks. I was probably as red as the apple my mom put in my lunch.

Ellie nudged my elbow and shot me a here's-your-chance-to-say-something-so-you'd-better-not-blow-it look.

I found my voice. "Hi, Justin."

Justin dug his hands into his jeans pockets. "Hey, Lexi."

The three of us stood there staring at each other. Talk about AWKWARD!

Finally, Justin broke the silence. "I'd better get to class."

"Me too. Bye." I lifted a hand to wave, when a group of rowdy kids roared past, shoving me forward. My hand landed on Justin's shoulder.

He grabbed my other hand and twirled me around, our faces inches apart. My heart beat fast and my knees wobbled. I couldn't believe I was dancing in the hall with

Justin Powell! At least it felt like we were dancing. What would it be like if there were music? My mind took a turn, and suddenly I was a princess in one of my mom's favorite Hallmark movies.

"What's this?" Bianca's voice screeched like fingernails on a chalkboard. "You know the 'no contact rule' during school hours. Do I need to tell my dad?" Bianca narrowed her eyes.

She's just jealous. The thought popped into my head as I stepped back, dropping my hands to my sides.

Bianca's three friends, who I call the Honey Bees, stood behind Bianca and nodded like bobblehead dolls.

"I saw the whole thing." Ellie cocked her head. "Justin was just trying to help. You shouldn't judge a situation when you don't know anything about it."

"Yeah, didn't you see?" Justin pointed down the hall. "Those kids almost ran us over."

I was proud of the way my friends stuck up for me, and yet I wished the gesture meant more to Justin than keeping me from landing on my behind.

"I'm not surprised." Bianca smiled at Justin. "You always did enjoy saving STRAYS. Remember that cute little kitten you gave me in elementary school?"

Was Bianca comparing me to a stray animal? OUCH.

"Actually," Justin said, "I found the kitten on the playground and brought it into the school office. Your dad just happened to be there to pick you up."

"Whatever." Bianca waved her hand in the air. She turned to her friends. "C'mon, girls. Let's go to class."

The girls followed Bianca down the hall like an entourage trailing their queen.

"We'd better hurry too, before the tardy bell rings," said Ellie.

"Thanks for holding me up." I grinned at Justin.

"No problem." He smiled back. "See ya around."

"Bye." I grabbed Ellie's arm and pulled her down the hall.

We stepped into Mrs. Dykstra's speech and drama class as the tardy bell rang.

"You two just made it. Please take a seat."

I dropped into a chair halfway down the middle row and set my backpack on the floor.

Ellie chose a seat toward the front, which didn't surprise me. She wants to be an actress and raises her hand every time Mrs. Dykstra asks for a volunteer.

I, on the other hand, always duck my head and hide behind the girl sitting in front of me, hoping to blend in with the crowd.

"Okay, class, quiet down. We need to start our 'Get to Know Me' speeches. Remember, don't read off your note cards, and keep it to approximately three minutes. I hope you all brought a visual aid. Let's start with Ellie." Mrs. Dykstra grinned at her.

Some kids called Ellie teacher's pet, but I know it's because she always pays attention and makes it known that she LOVES the class.

In her speech, Ellie talked about how she is the oldest of six kids, has lived in the same two-story house her whole life, and took an amazing trip to Hawaii with her family this past summer. Her visual aid was a PowerPoint

presentation, and she flipped through the pictures as she spoke. All the kids were drawn in, me included.

Ten students gave their speeches before it was my turn. My mouth suddenly felt as dry as my morning toast. I tried to swallow, but I couldn't get past the lump lodged in my throat. Maybe nerves made my tonsils grow. Pretty soon I wouldn't be able to breathe. Before I fell over from asphyxiation, the bell rang.

Phew! That was close. Now I'd have more time to practice and figure out a way to stay calm. But that also meant I had another night to worry myself to sleep.

Ellie approached me as I gathered my things and put them in my backpack. "Too bad. It was your turn."

"Yeah, too bad," I repeated. Ellie didn't need to know how anxious I felt. "I'll see you at break. Save me a spot in the quad."

"We can only go to the quad if Abby is here today," Ellie warned. "If not, we're out of luck."

Abby made the volleyball team, which boosted her to popularity status. Without her, we'd get the stare-down from the jocks and popular girls. Nothing is worse!

Of course Bianca and her friends hang out in the quad EVERY day.

"I'll meet you by the lockers," I said. "And we'll follow Abby to the quad."

"That's a plan." Ellie gave me a high five before moving to the next class.

It's not as if we're using Abby. After all, we're okay with standing by the basketball court or water fountain, where the losers and average kids stand.

Yeah, right!

I want more than anything to know what it feels like to be popular.

All during math class, my mind wandered. If Abby moves away, I'll only have one best friend at school. And if something happens to Ellie, I'll have no one. My thoughts were spinning out of control, and I didn't like where they were taking me.

The sound of Justin's voice brought me back to the present. "Do you have an eraser I can borrow?"

I gladly handed him my pencil. "But I need it back when you're done. It's my only one."

He erased his answer and gave it back. "Sorry about what happened earlier. Bianca can be so . . ." He shook his head and let his words hang in midair.

Thoughtless. Mean. Self-centered. I filled the blank in my head.

"Insecure," he finally said.

Now that was a word I wasn't expecting. How can Justin be so blind? He has no idea what he's talking about. Bianca has more confidence than a pack of wolves. "Really? Why would you say that?"

Mr. Baxter cut into our conversation. "Please be quiet and focus on your work."

I chewed on my pencil, one of my bad habits whenever I feel anxious. By the time math ended, I was no closer to finding out why Justin thinks Bianca is insecure. Does he know something I don't?

Personally, I think Bianca loves making people squirm, and for some reason I happen to be her target this year.

I wanted to catch up with Justin after class and ask him what he meant, but he started talking with some of his friends and I lost my chance. I moved down the hall toward my locker to meet Ellie.

Suddenly I wanted to hang out in the quad more than ever.

Love, Lexi 🖤

Dear Lexi,
Don't worry about anything; instead, pray about every-thing. Tell Me what you need, and remember to thank Me for all I have done. Then you will experience My peace, which exceeds anything you can understand. My peace will guard your heart and mind. (Philippians 4:6-7)
Love, God

Trust in God

When we worry, it feels like we're doing something useful—but we aren't. Truth is, worrying is never constructive. It won't solve your problems or give you answers. Instead of worrying, pray about your situation and trust God to take care of you. He will give you peace.

What's YOUR Story?

Dear God,

I'm really worried. Here's what's happening:

_____

_____

_____

_____

_____

_____

_____

_____

_____

_____

_____

_____

_____

_____

_____

_____

_____

_____

_____

_____

_____

_____

_____

I can show my trust in you by . . .

_____

_____

_____

_____

_____

_____

_____

_____

_____

_____

_____

_____

_____

_____

_____

_____

_____

_____

_____

Thank you for all you have done for me. Help me to pray about everything!

Love, _____

You will keep in perfect peace
all who trust in you,
all whose thoughts are fixed on you!
Isaiah 26:3

Friday, September 9

Dear God,

For the last two days, Ellie and I have been hanging out in the quad with Abby and the popular kids during lunch. It felt good to be part of the in crowd—until today, when Bianca made a TOTAL scene!

Here's what happened.

From her special spot at the far picnic table, Bianca called out to Abby and gestured her over with a nod of her head.

"I'd better see what she wants." Abby grabbed her bagged lunch and joined Bianca and the Honey Bees.

The second Abby walked away, I knew Bianca was up to no good. She had never given Abby the time of day. What did Bianca want with one of my best friends?

I didn't want to stare, but I couldn't help myself. My sandwich lodged in my throat as I watched Abby share her bag of chips with Bianca and her cohorts.

Suddenly, Bianca stood, grabbed her soda from the table, and waltzed over to where Ellie and I were sitting. "What are you two doing here?" she hissed. "Don't you belong on the other side of the school with the freaks and geeks?"

I swallowed hard, took a swig from my water bottle, and grinned, pretending to be more confident than I felt. "We're here with Abby."

Bianca shook her head and pointed across the quad. "Oh no, you're not. Abby's over there."

"Well, she was here a minute ago," Ellie said.

"Yeah, until you called her over," I added.

"The only reason Abby is in the quad is because she made the volleyball team. And the ONLY reason I called her over is because I wanted some of her chips."

I balled my hands into fists, wanting to punch Bianca for talking about my friend that way. But hitting has never solved anything, even though it would've made me feel good . . . for about a nanosecond. Instead, I decided to ignore her and her hurtful words, and I turned away.

Apparently this annoyed Bianca BIG TIME!

The next thing I knew, Ellie's eyes grew big and round, and something cold and wet slithered down my hair and face. Bianca had dumped her soda on my head in front of all the popular kids in the quad!

Laughter erupted all around us.

I could not believe she did that! For what felt like a really long time, I just sat there, frozen. It felt like my mind had actually gone blank with shock.

Then I bit my lip, stopping myself from crying or saying something I would regret later, and mopped my face with a napkin. I don't know how I was able to stay so calm! Were you helping me, God? Is that what you mean by a peace that exceeds anything I can understand?

Bianca shot Ellie a warning look. "You're next if you don't get out of here."

I pushed my frizzy, sticky hair away from my face. "We're not going anywhere."

"Yeah." Ellie scooted down the bench, out of Bianca's reach, and popped a grape in her mouth.

Bianca tipped the soda can upside down. She stared at us, her eyes like two daggers. "You're lucky it's gone."

My face was still wet and sticky, but I wouldn't let Bianca have the satisfaction of seeing me wipe it again. "Luck has nothing to do with it."

Abby joined us at the table. "Leave my friends alone. They have every right to be here, same as you."

Way to go, Abby!

The thought zipped through my mind right before the Honey Bees approached and stood behind their Queen. Yikes! I imagined arms and fists flying—and how much trouble I'd be in if we ended up in a fight.

Instead, Bianca put her hands on her hips and said, "Ellie and Lexi have to earn their way into the quad."

I could say the same for the girls standing next to Bianca, but I decided to keep quiet. As my mom would say, why ruffle her feathers?

Abby stood and motioned to Ellie and me. "Come on, girls. We don't need this."

Were we really going to leave the quad because of Bianca?

Part of me wanted to go, but another part wanted to face up to the PD and tell her what I really thought of her. That's when Justin's words from a couple of days ago started bouncing around in my head.

"Bianca can be so . . . insecure."

I don't know if he's right, but I do know that she likes to be in control of the whole school—even who gets to hang out in the quad. I wonder what would happen if I reported Bianca's behavior to a teacher or HER DAD!!!

(Besides, we're not even allowed to have soda at school. How does Bianca always get away with stuff?)

After we grabbed our backpacks, Abby stepped between Ellie and me and linked arms with us. As we walked away, I heard giggles and whispers. I bet I could guess what the popular kids were saying. And none of it was good! I'd never be able to show my face in the quad again.

Unless . . .

Suddenly, an idea formed. There was a way we could hang out in the quad at lunch, but it would take a miracle . . . and more courage than I have.

Last week at church I heard our pastor say, "With God all things are possible." Is that true?

Love, Lexi ♡

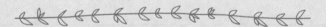

Dear Lexi,
If you have faith even as small as a mustard seed, you could say to this mountain, "Move from here to there," and it would move. Nothing would be impossible.
(Matthew 17:20)
Love, God

A Bit of Faith

God is BIG and can handle BIG things. Nothing is too hard for Him. You can pray to Him about *anything,* because He is bigger than any problems you may face. All you need are courage and a little bit of faith. With God, all things are possible!

What's YOUR Story?

Dear God,

Right now life seems impossible. Here's why:

_____

_____

_____

_____

_____

_____

_____

_____

I can give the situation to you by . . .

_____

_____

_____

_____

_____

_____

_____

_____

_____

_____

Thank you for being a BIG God! Help me to have faith.

Love, _____

Jesus . . . said, "Humanly speaking, it is impossible.
But with God everything is possible."
Matthew 19:26

Sunday, September 11

Dear God,

All weekend long I've been thinking about what happened in the quad on Friday.

My sister laughed when I told her the story. "So, what did you do?" she asked. "Walk around with soda in your hair all afternoon?"

"No." I curled my lip and rolled my eyes. "I went to the girls' locker room and stuck my head under the faucet. Duh!"

Thank goodness Mom wasn't in our room. She would've grounded me for a week for my sassy attitude.

Kate laughed some more.

"It's not funny." I flopped back on my bed. "How would you like it if it happened to you?"

"Things like that don't happen to me," Kate said.

I turned my back toward Kate. She has no idea what it's like to be me.

My idea to hang out in the quad was becoming clearer. Yes, it would take a miracle, but I had to do something drastic for Bianca and her friends to accept me, and Ellie, as part of the popular crowd.

"You know, being popular isn't that great," Kate said, her voice sounding oddly nice. "There's a lot of pressure to be cool."

"I wouldn't know, would I?" The moment I let the words shoot out of my mouth, I regretted them. Why did I ruin the nice-sister moment?

"I just thought I'd save you the trouble and humiliation of wanting what you'll never have." Kate went back to her usual sarcastic self.

"Whatever!" I pushed my face into my pillow. Deep down, I know what Kate said is true. Being popular must have its drawbacks. But until I get a chance to experience what it's like to be popular, I'm not going to give up trying.

"Girls," Mom called to us from the bottom of the stairs. "Remember, Dad and I are going out to dinner. There are sandwiches in the refrigerator. Please keep an eye on your brother."

"Okay," Kate called back. "Have a good time."

Does Mom really think Kate watches Ben while they're away? She always makes some excuse, like she has home-work, wants to paint her fingernails, or needs to call a friend. I always make sure Ben eats dinner, gets in his pajamas, and brushes his teeth before bed. Tonight wasn't going to be any different.

An hour later the doorbell rang.

I peeked through the window. My heart nearly stopped when I saw Justin Powell standing on the other side of the door. What was he doing at my house?

Ben rushed to the door and opened it. He's not allowed to, but I wasn't going to yell at him in front of my crush!

"What do you want?" Ben kept his hand on the knob. Was he going to slam the door in Justin's face?

I scooted next to my brother. "Ben, don't talk to Justin that way." I gave him a sheepish grin. "You can come in."

Justin shook his head. "No, that's okay. I didn't know you lived here."

Really? Bummer! "Then what are you doing here?"

Justin smiled and shrugged a shoulder. "I'm going door-to-door selling chocolate and cookie dough."

"Did I hear someone say chocolate?" Kate appeared from her bedroom. Why did she have to come out now?

"Yes, but you can buy chocolate from me." I looked directly at her and narrowed my eyes. Would Kate get the hint?

"Wait a minute," Kate said, pointing one of her newly painted fingernails. "Did I hear you say your name is Justin? Lexi always talks about you." She winked at me. "He's cute."

Did Kate really say that out loud? UGH! My face and neck heated up.

"Why don't you go with Justin and sell around the neighborhood?" Kate grinned. "I'll keep an eye on Ben."

I couldn't believe my ears! Was my sister actually telling me to sell chocolate and cookie dough with Justin Powell? Was I dreaming?

Then reality hit. What if he didn't want me to go with him?

"Do you mind?" I asked Justin, giving him my best smile.

"It's cool, but I have to be home in an hour."

A whole hour with my crush! Perfect.

I just didn't count on Dylan and Ryan showing up five minutes later.

"What's up?" Dylan asked.

"Yeah, how come she's selling with you?" Ryan folded his arms across his chest and raised his chin in the air.

All of a sudden I wanted to disappear behind the neighbor's hydrangea bush.

Justin shrugged a shoulder. "Lexi's all right. She can sell with us."

"But we each won't sell as much with her along." Ryan followed behind us, his words like a knife to my back.

"Yeah," Dylan said. "And then we might not win the grand prize."

"I have an idea," Justin said. "You guys go down that street." He gestured to the left. "And Lexi and I will take this one."

"Oh, I get it. You two want to be ALONE. Come on, Dylan," Ryan said, tugging on his friend's arm. "Let's go."

"Wait. I'll go home." It took every ounce of willpower to say those words, but I didn't want to cause a fight.

Justin shook his head. "You don't have to go."

"Yes, I do," I said. "Your friends don't want me around."

Ryan and Dylan grinned at each other.

"Look, we're all friends," Justin said. "Why don't we hang out at the park? I'm tired of selling this stuff anyway. Aren't you?"

I had barely started, but I wasn't going to argue.

Dylan nudged Ryan. "C'mon. Let's sell on the next street over and let Justin and Lexi go down this one. It's no big deal."

Ryan rolled his eyes. "Okay. See you guys later."

Once they left, Justin and I stared awkwardly at each other. I tried to think of something to say.

Then a car zoomed past. I jerked my head around in time to see my parents' van pulling into our driveway. How come they were home already? I glanced at my watch. I'd only had fifteen minutes with Justin, and even less time selling chocolate and cookie dough.

But I wasn't about to get in trouble AGAIN!

"Gotta run!" I took off down the street, leaving Justin alone on the sidewalk. I slipped into the house through the front door.

Now as I lie in bed writing this letter, I realize something. In addition to having mesmerizing blue eyes, Justin is a really nice guy. No wonder I like him so much.

Sweet dreams. Guess who I'll be dreaming about? His initials are JP!!!!!!!!!!!!!!!!!!!!!!

Love, Lexi

Dear Lexi,
Love is patient and kind. Love is not jealous or boastful or proud or rude. It does not demand its own way. It is not irritable, and it keeps no record of being wronged. It does not rejoice about injustice but rejoices whenever the truth wins out. Love never gives up, never loses faith, is always hopeful, and endures through every circumstance. (1 Corinthians 13:4–7)
Love, God

True Love

Do you have a crush? Is there a certain boy who makes you feel shy, embarrassed, or giddy inside? Of course God wants you to follow your parents' rules about dating and having a boyfriend. But He knows that it's normal for you to think someone is special. After all, He made you to want to love and be loved! But He wants you to keep the proper perspective. Whether your crush likes you or not, the important thing is to be his friend and keep God number one in your life—because He loves you most of all.

What's YOUR Story?

Dear God,

I have a crush on a boy. Here's how it started:

_____

_____

_____

_____

_____

_____

_____

_____

_____

_____

_____

_____

I can keep You number one in my life by . . .

_____

_____

_____

_____

_____

_____

_____

_____

_____

_____

_____

_____

_____

Thank you for loving me. Help me to love others like you do.

Love, _____

Three things will last forever—faith, hope, and love—and the greatest of these is love.
1 Corinthians 13:13

Monday, September 12

Dear God,

I think we should skip Mondays because everyone walks around like zombies.

This morning, my dad poured juice over his cereal instead of milk. I laughed REALLY LOUD, and then apologized when he gave me a stern look. It must not have sounded sincere, because he sent me to my room for being disrespectful. I wanted to tell him to lighten up, but I knew if I said that, I'd be grounded for the rest of the year! Instead, I walked into our bedroom to find Kate still in bed.

"Wake up!" I yelled through Kate's cheerleading megaphone. She jumped a mile and banged her head on the bedpost. How should I know sound traveled so well through that thing? Oops!

"You're going to get it." She sprang out of bed and chased me down the hall.

"MOM!" I screamed. "Help!"

Right then Ben walked into the hallway in his dinosaur pajamas, dragging his blanket behind him. I nearly smacked into him, but sidestepped at the last minute.

Kate wasn't as quick. BAM! She and Ben rammed into each other and fell to the floor.

Mom raced out of her bedroom wearing her fuzzy blue robe, her hair sticking out every which way like she hadn't brushed it yet. She picked Ben up and hugged him. "Are you all right, sweetie?"

53

He nodded.

"What about me?" Kate lay on the floor, clutching her hip.

I stood in the corner of the hallway, hoping my mom wouldn't notice me, which shouldn't be hard. I am the invisible middle child, right?

Not today! Mom glared at me like she already knew the collision was my fault. "Lexi, what happened?"

"Well . . . Kate and Ben smacked into each other and fell down." It was the truth.

Dad stomped up the stairs. "What now? Lexi, you're supposed to be in your room—"

"I was, until Kate chased me—"

"Because you woke me up and made me bang my head."

"You're the one who ran into Ben," I said.

"Well, I wouldn't have if you hadn't woken me up!"

"I wouldn't have woken you up if Dad hadn't sent me to my room." I knew I was pushing it.

"Hold on there a minute." Dad stopped me with a hand. "You shouldn't have been disrespectful when I poured juice on my cereal."

"You did what?" Mom asked, stifling a giggle.

"I poured juice . . ." Dad smirked. "Okay, it is kind of funny."

Now that everyone was fully awake, I was glad I wasn't the only one laughing. Even Kate smiled at me after I told her I was sorry for waking her up the way I did. We had a fun family moment until Dad looked at his watch and announced we had ten minutes to get to the bus stop!

YIKES!

Since I was already dressed, I helped Ben while Mom scrambled to make our lunches. We made the bus with a minute to spare, and before long I was sitting in the middle row in speech and drama class.

Mrs. Dykstra walked up and down the aisles, handing out grades for our first speech. It's been four days since I finally gave mine. My knees shook and I felt like I was going to throw up, but once I started talking, the experience wasn't as bad as I thought . . . until I got my evaluation back! A big, red letter C filled the top right corner.

Ellie sat directly in front of me today. I bet I know exactly what grade she got, not that I'm jealous or anything. Ellie is a natural-born actress and could fake her way through a speech and get a better grade than me ANY day.

She swiveled to face me. "What did you get?"

"C as in cat," I said, shoving my paper inside my notebook. I wasn't in the mood to read the teacher's comments.

"Meet me after class," Ellie said. "I have something to tell you."

Whenever Ellie says something like that, it usually means something BIG is going on. I glanced at the clock. How was I going to survive another 45 minutes? I was going to need a whole lot of patience to last all through class without knowing Ellie's secret.

For a while I tried to concentrate on what Mrs. Dykstra was saying, but eventually I couldn't stand it anymore. I had to know the secret NOW!

I tore off the corner of a piece of paper and

scribbled a quick note across the top. After folding it in half, I tossed it over Ellie's shoulder. Thank goodness it landed on her desk.

Instead of reading the note, Ellie raised her hand and asked to be excused to the restroom.

Was this a ploy to get out of class? That didn't make sense. Ellie loved speech and drama. Or did she want me to follow her so she could tell me what was going on? My heart pounded.

The second Ellie left, I wanted to snatch the note off her desk. If Dylan shifted in his seat, Mrs. Dykstra was sure to see it.

"Alexis, it's your turn to read." Mrs. Dykstra's voice cut into my thoughts.

When I heard my name, my breath caught in my throat. I hadn't even opened my copy of the play **Snow White**. Giggles erupted around me, and my face felt as though it were a hundred degrees.

Maybe I should've stayed home and hidden under the covers. Today was definitely a Monday, and I was the worst zombie of all. But then how would I find out Ellie's secret?

"Page 4, halfway down," Mrs. Dykstra directed. "Please read to the bottom of the next page starting where the wicked queen says, 'Mirror! Mirror on the wall! Who is the fairest of them all?'"

At first my voice shook as I read, but then I cleared my throat and pretended to have Ellie's confidence. Pretty soon I was so focused on the characters that I didn't care that thirty kids were listening to my EVERY word. Well, almost. My voice hitched as I read the last line.

"Thank you, Alexis. Great job." Mrs. Dykstra smiled at me and called on another student to pick up where I left off.

I admit it felt good to get a compliment! Maybe I have an ounce of acting talent.

The bell rang. All the kids slammed their books and raced out the door.

Where was Ellie?

I snagged the note sitting in the middle of her desk, along with her backpack.

Ellie walked in the classroom and grinned. "So how'd you do?"

"What do you mean?"

"I left so that it would be your turn to read."

My eyes glazed over as I repeated Ellie's words in my head. "You're telling me you left class on purpose?"

"So that you wouldn't have a chance to get nervous." Ellie blinked like she had an eye twitch. "Are you mad?"

I shook my head. "But the note. Didn't you see it?"

Ellie scrunched up her nose. "What note?"

"This one." I opened my hand to show her the small wad of paper. "I tossed it onto your desk right before you left to go to the bathroom. By the way, what took you so long?"

Ellie ignored my question, unfolded the piece of paper, and read the three words I scribbled in capital letters. **TELL ME NOW!** She laughed. "I was going to tell you right after class. It's really no big deal."

"So?" I held up my hands. "What's up?"

"Your mom didn't tell you?" Ellie glanced at the floor, her shoulders slumping a little.

"Why would my mom know your secret?" I twisted the strap of my backpack, getting more restless by the minute.

"She is the receptionist at the optometrist's office."

"Do you need glasses or something? Is that the real reason you skipped out of class?" I could put two and two together, but I'd rather Ellie just come right out and say it.

"You do get nervous." Ellie's voice sounded small. "But I can't see the words clearly."

"Don't worry, your secret is safe with me."

"Yeah, until it's obvious."

"Hey, glasses are a fashion statement. It's in all the magazines. Besides, you'll look great." I pulled Ellie down the hall.

I have a secret of my own. I haven't told Ellie about my idea to get us back in the quad, but encouraging my best friend is more important.

Love, Lexi ♡

Dear Lexi,
Encourage each other and build each other up, just as you are already doing. (1 Thessalonians 5:11)
Love, God

Encourage Others

When a friend is going through hard times, it's important to listen and offer encouragement. When you do this, you're not only helping your friend, but you are demonstrating God's love. And guess what? Encouraging others makes you feel good about yourself, too!

What's YOUR Story?

Dear God,

I have a friend who needs encouragement. Here's what's happening:

_____

_____

_____

_____

_____

_____

_____

_____

_____

I can say words that are good and helpful, such as . . .

_____

_____

_____

_____

_____

_____

_____

_____

_____

_____

_____

_____

Thank you for my friends. Help me to encourage and build them up.

Love, _____

Let everything you say be good and
helpful, so that your words will be an
encouragement to those who hear them.
Ephesians 4:29

CHOCOLATE

Tuesday, September 13

Hey, God!

Ellie and Abby told me today that my big idea of having a dance performance at the school assembly where they would announce the winners of the chocolate-selling competition was CRAZY, especially because I wanted Bianca on the team.

Didn't they understand the point of the dance team was to boost us to popular status so that we could hang out in the quad with the cool kids?

"Easy for you to say, Abby. You can go to the quad any time you want." I slurped from the water fountain so that I didn't have to make eye contact with my two "best" friends.

Abby curled her upper lip. "But to purposefully invite the PD? That's nuts!"

"How do we know she's not going to kick us out or that she'll allow us to be part of the dance team in the first place?" Ellie asked.

"Mrs. Dykstra, that's how." I smirked. "I talked with her after class, and she said she was proud of me for wanting to start a dance group and that she'd help in any way she can."

"Good thinking." Ellie grinned.

"See, it's not so crazy after all." I folded my arms across my chest. It seemed I had won Ellie over.

But her smile faded. "The dance group is a good idea, but I agree with Abby. No Bianca."

61

Personally, I can't dance very well. Why would I choose to make a fool of myself in public unless I had someone like Bianca to teach me? There's no way I'm going to do this unless the best dancer of the ENTIRE school is a part of it, even if she is mean. I can handle a couple of weeks of torture to be popular the rest of the year!

"I can't stop her if she wants to join." I shrugged a shoulder and pretended I needed something from my backpack, hoping to get Ellie and Abby off my back.

I doubted Abby wanted to be on the dance team anyway because of volleyball. Besides, she doesn't care whether or not she is popular, which is TOTALLY ironic since she's the baby of her family and is used to getting all the attention.

Ellie and I, on the other hand, need all the help we can get! I know Ellie wants to hang out in the quad as much as I do.

Before we left school, we agreed not to talk about the dance group until tomorrow, but since I'm the one who thought up the idea, I decided to take things into my own hands. Abby and Ellie will just have to go along with my plan.

"What are you doing?" Kate plopped on her bed the minute she came home from school.

Why is it that if I asked her the same thing, she'd roll her eyes at me, tell me to buzz off, or treat me like gum on the bottom of her shoe?

I continued coloring bubble words in bright Crayola colors. "Making a sign for the dance team tryouts." I said it like it was an everyday occurrence.

Kate bolted to a sitting position. "Dance team? Don't tell me you're going to try out." She covered a laugh.

"I don't have to try out, because I'm the captain of the team. The whole thing is my idea."

"Really?" Kate widened her eyes so big I thought her eyeballs were going to pop out of their sockets.

I admired my sign and turned it to face Kate. "Don't believe me? Look for yourself."

MRS. DYKSTRA'S DANCE TEAM
Tryouts Friday, September 16, after school
Captain: Alexis Cooper
What? Group of six dancers
Where? School gymnasium
Why? To promote school spirit
When? Performance September 30, before the announcement of the WINNERS of the pizza lunch and limo ride!
Come be a part of this popular team!

"You've got to be kidding me." Kate shook her head.

I tucked the sign-up sheet in a folder and stuffed it in my backpack. "I'm completely serious."

"Who's going to want to be on your dance team? Once they see you're the captain, they'll run the other way."

I never thought Bianca might not want to try out.

Another thought zoomed through my head. As captain, I would be in charge. And I barely know my right foot from my left. Without Bianca, we'd look like TOTAL idiots. Suddenly, things were going from bad to worse.

Until dinner . . .

Over spaghetti and meatballs, Dad mentioned he'll be out of town for a week at a big business convention. That means we'll all have to pick up the slack, like take out the garbage and make sure Mom doesn't go crazy taking care of us kids. We've been through this a bazillion times since Dad travels a lot selling life insurance. Why do grown-ups need that stuff, anyway?

"Will you be home on September 30?" I stabbed at my noodles with a fork and twirled, then stuck the wad of spaghetti in my mouth.

"I think so. Why?" Dad asked between bites. "What's happening on the thirtieth?"

Kate answered before I had a chance. "Lexi's going to dance."

"Really?" Mom smiled and her eyes lit up. Her response was similar to Kate's, and yet I felt more hopeful inside.

"Yep," I said. "I'm in charge of a dance team, and we're performing at the school assembly before they announce who sold the most chocolate and cookie dough."

As I said the words, it hit me. If I learned to dance AND won the grand prize, I might become more popular than Bianca! Girls would follow ME around school like I was royalty.

"Lexi, I'm really proud of you," Mom said. "I'm sure Kate will help you—won't you, honey?"

"Well, I, er . . ." Suddenly my older sister had nothing to say!

I jumped in before she thought of something sarcastic. "Thanks, Kate."

With or without Bianca, performing at the assembly will get me noticed—by the students AND my family. I bit into a meatball and grinned. What could go wrong?

Love, Lexi 🖤

Dear Lexi,
Humble yourself before Me, and I will lift you up in honor. (James 4:10)
Love, God

Pride vs. Humility

Are you proud or humble? While prideful people think of themselves first and not enough about others, those who are humble look out for others, are not selfish, and do not try to impress people. God wants His children to be humble, because pride gets in the way of loving Him and others. Focus on glorifying God's name, and let Him take care of your reputation.

What's YOUR Story?

Dear God,

I want everyone to think I'm cool, because . . .

_____

_____

_____

_____

_____

_____

_____

_____

_____

_____

_____

_____

_____

_____

I can be humble by . . .

_____

_____

_____

_____

_____

_____

_____

_____

_____

_____

_____

_____

_____

_____

Thank you for showing me how to be humble. Help me to
bring glory to your name.

Love, _____

Pride leads to disgrace,
but with humility comes wisdom.
Proverbs 11:2

Wednesday, September 14

Dear God,

My WORST nightmare came true!

Someone crossed off my name as dance team captain and replaced it with Bianca's. And the Honey Bees were first on the sign-up list for the dance group tryouts.

How could my amazing, wonderful, awesome idea go so horribly wrong? And now I had to listen to Abby and Ellie say, "I told you so."

At the end of the school day, Justin was walking by as I snatched the sign-up from the bulletin board and wadded it up in a ball.

"Whoa. What's the matter?" He dug his hands in his jeans pockets.

I shoved the paper into my backpack. "It's not worth talking about."

"C'mon. It can't be that bad."

I clenched my jaw. "How would you like it if your idea was stolen from you?"

Justin shrugged a shoulder. "Depends, I guess."

"Hmm." I thought for a few seconds. "What if you wanted to be captain of the football team and someone swooped in and took it from you?"

"To be captain of the football team you have to be voted in," Justin said.

"Okay, bad example." I racked my brain, trying to think of another one. "Okay, I got it. What if you wanted to start a band, and you made a sign saying you were the lead guitar player, and someone crossed your name off and wrote their name instead?"

"Wow, really? Who crossed off your name?" Justin lifted his hand to stop me from answering. "Let me guess. Bianca?"

"Yep." Air puffed between my lips. "I wanted her to sign up, but I didn't think she'd replace me as captain."

"Are you sure it was her? Maybe it was somebody else."

Justin did have a point. I didn't actually see her do it. "My guess is either Bianca or one of the Honey Bees."

"Honey Bees?" Justin furrowed his brow.

Justin didn't know the nickname Abby, Ellie, and I had for Bianca's entourage. "Yeah, Bianca's friends—Olivia, Isabella, and Sophia." I hadn't realized all their names ended in the letter A until that moment.

Justin chuckled. "You're funny, Lexi."

"I'm glad you find my situation so hilarious—"

"I'm sorry. I didn't mean to laugh." Justin straightened his face. "Can I see your sign?"

Could I trust him not to make fun of me for wanting to be captain of the dance group? I wouldn't be able to stand it if he thought my idea was crazy, like Ellie and Abby did.

He must have noticed my hesitation, because he stepped toward me and said, "Please?"

I couldn't believe my school crush was begging me to show him my idea—something that meant so much to me. My stomach felt jittery and my hands started to sweat. I rubbed them down the sides of my jeans, then opened my bag and rummaged through my stuff.

My cheeks burned when I found the crinkled paper. I

had worked a long time on that sign, making it neat and colorful, and now it was a wadded-up mess. I handed the paper ball to Justin. He unfolded it and then flattened it against his shirt. The sweet gesture made me smile.

"A dance group, huh?"

"Yeah, I know, it's a stupid idea."

Justin shook his head. "No, it's not. Sounds like fun. Can guys join?"

I grinned. "You're kidding, right?"

"Yeah." He smiled.

How did Justin get such perfectly straight teeth without braces? Must be nice. I closed my lips around my brackets. Maybe it would be better if I kept my mouth shut.

Justin continued, "Everyone knows Bianca has danced since she learned to walk. She talks about it all the time. Anyone could've put her name down as captain."

Did the whole school think Bianca should be captain? My shoulders sagged. As hard as Justin was trying to make me feel better, suddenly I felt WORSE.

Justin's eyes met mine. "What about making Bianca a cocaptain?"

Did I want to share the limelight with Bianca Taylor when it was my idea in the first place? I bit my lip.

Justin handed me the sign and shrugged a shoulder. "Think about it. See you around, Lexi."

I raised my hand to wave, but Justin had already walked off.

God, would you cross my name off the list too?

Love, Lexi ♡

Dear Lexi,
Be strong and courageous! Do not be afraid or discour-
aged. For I am with you wherever you go. (Joshua 1:9)
Love, God

Strong and Courageous

Discouragement can happen when you least expect it, especially when you are hungry, frustrated, sad, or tired. Before you do something you shouldn't, like take your feelings out on someone else, remember to eat every few hours, talk to a trustworthy friend or adult when you need to unload, and get lots of sleep. And don't forget to pray! Everyone has bad days, so you are not alone. God is with you and will make you strong!

What's YOUR Story?

Dear God,

I'm so discouraged. Here's what's going on:

_____

_____

But I know you are with me, because . . .

Thank you for being with me wherever I go. Help me to put my hope in YOU!

Love, _____

Why am I discouraged?
Why is my heart so sad?
I will put my hope in God!
Psalm 42:5

Thursday, September 15

Dear God,

Mom's been stressed out with Dad out of town. How do I know? Because the minute I came home from school, she said she couldn't be at two places at once and made me hang out with Ben at a birthday party while she ran errands.

Apparently we were out of EVERYTHING, including bread and milk, two things I can't live without. (How am I going to make peanut butter sandwiches or chocolate milk without the main ingredients?)

So I agreed to go to the party even if it meant I would have to stay up late to do my homework.

Mom dropped us off at Hannah's house, and Ben hid behind me while I rang the doorbell. I thought he might be embarrassed because he was dressed like a super-hero, until Hannah answered the door wearing a princess costume, complete with crown and plastic high heels. I wanted to tell them Halloween is next month, but appar-ently that doesn't matter to five-year-olds.

"C'mon, Ben." Hannah motioned him inside. "Come see my cake. It's a castle." They took off running, and I was left in the entrance feeling out of place.

To be completely honest, I had another motive for going to the birthday party. Twenty kindergartners equal twenty moms or dads hopefully willing to buy a tub of cookie dough or a box of chocolate. Their sweet, ador-able (and sometimes annoying) children would one day be in middle school, and who wouldn't want their kids to experience up-to-date technology in the form of state-of-the-art computers? (Don't I sound smart? I wrote down what my homeroom teacher said, and it's sure to amaze the grown-ups.) The catalog and order forms for the school-wide fund-raiser were tucked inside the bag hanging from my shoulder.

I wasn't there two minutes before I found Winnie-the-Pooh crying. Of course it wasn't really Winnie-the-Pooh, but a freckle-faced boy searching for his mom. I patted his fuzzy head and told him I'd help him find her. Maybe she'd buy some chocolate or cookie dough to thank me for helping her son.

Instead I ran into Olivia, one of Bianca's Honey Bees, leading a game of Duck, Duck, Goose.

"What are you doing here?" she asked in a surprisingly friendly voice.

"I'm here with my brother, Ben." I pointed to the boy across the room wearing a cape.

"Hannah's my cousin," Olivia said. "After the party, my family's going out to dinner to celebrate."

I was shocked that one of the Honey Bees was even talking to me. Olivia seemed a lot nicer away from school.

"Do you know where I can find his mom?" I gestured to the little kid by my side.

"Have you checked the kitchen? That's where most of the adults are hanging out." Olivia glanced over her shoulder at the wiggly kindergartners waiting for her to play Duck, Duck, Goose. "Hey, kid, get back in the circle."

That sounded more like the Olivia who went to Green Acres Middle School.

"See you later." I laid a hand on Winnie-the-Pooh's shoulder and led him to the kitchen.

A minute later the boy sat on his mom's lap, and my chance to sell chocolate and cookie dough had arrived.

I sat on the stool beside the child's mom and pulled out the catalog and order forms. Suddenly my mouth dried up and the words stuck in my throat.

"What do you have there?" the pretty brown-haired woman asked, pushing my awkwardness aside.

"Want to buy some chocolate and cookie dough to support Green Acres Middle School? It's for new computers." My lips quivered. Maybe I do need Kate or someone to help me. This selling stuff is nerve racking.

"Let me take a look." She shifted her son to her other knee and thumbed through the catalog. Before long she had ordered a tub of snickerdoodle cookie dough and a box of assorted chocolates.

Soon all the adults in the kitchen had made an order. As my form filled up, I daydreamed about the limo ride and pizza lunch I was sure to win—until Olivia walked into the kitchen and put a halt to any more orders.

"The birthday girl is MY relative. Shouldn't they order from ME?" Her hands were on her hips, and she wore a scowl on her face.

Whoops! Olivia may have had a point.

"I'm done." I slipped the catalog and order form into my shoulder bag, then scooted off the stool to look for my brother. Sure, we'd only been there thirty minutes, but I was ready to leave.

I found Ben sitting at a small table in the corner of the family room, coloring with three other kids. I leaned down. "Ready to go?"

Ben shook his head. He licked his lips and stared at his paper in deep concentration.

"C'mon, Ben. I've got homework. Mom said we could walk home if we left before dark." Funny how Mom won't let me sell door-to-door by myself, but she allows me to be responsible for a five-year-old child.

"But we didn't have cake. Hannah said it was chocolate." Ben looked at me out of the corner of his eye and gave me a lopsided grin.

Even my brother knows my weakness for chocolate. "Okay, fine. But after we eat cake, we're leaving." I clutched my bag. There was no way I was going to let those orders out of my sight.

What I hadn't counted on was Bianca showing up at the party. I licked the last bit of chocolate frosting off my fork, my stomach twisting into a queasy knot. Olivia whispered something into Bianca's ear, and I grasped the handle of my bag, holding it close to my side.

My heart skipped a beat when Bianca walked toward me. I had avoided her all day at school because of the dance team captain fiasco, and suddenly I had no choice but to face her.

I felt a tug on the hem of my shirt.

"Lexi, can you take me to the bathroom?" Ben hopped from one foot to the other.

Perfect timing!

I wrapped an arm around his shoulders and bolted down the hall in search of the restroom. By the time we came out, Mom was standing in the entrance.

"Hey, Mom, ready to go?" I looped my arm in hers and pulled her to the front door.

"Hold on, Alexis. Hannah is opening presents. I'm sure Ben wants to watch."

"You don't want to see a bunch of girl stuff, do you?" I tried to use my most convincing voice, but it didn't seem to matter.

Ben skipped to the group of kids and plopped down on the floor.

"Lexi, it'll only take a minute." Mom weaved to the corner of the room.

Yeah, it would only take a minute for Bianca or Olivia to come over and snatch the order forms too!

Or say something mean.

I inched closer to Mom, wedging my bag between us. No matter what, I had to protect what was rightfully mine.

"Aren't those girls in your class?" Mom asked. "I think they want to talk with you. They keep looking our way."

I didn't want Mom to know how much those girls intimidated me, so I did what any confident junior high girl would do, even though I was shaking inside.

"Can you hold this? I'll be right back." I handed Mom my bag, took a deep breath, and then walked over to where Bianca and Olivia stood. I pushed down the lump lodged in my throat and said, "Are you going to try out for the dance team tomorrow? I saw your names on the list."

"Why wouldn't we?" Olivia said. "We're the best dancers in school."

Bianca crossed her arms. "WHO is the best dancer?"

"Okay, Bianca is the best, but I'm good too." Olivia batted her lashes. "Right?"

"Of course you are, but not as good as me." Bianca sent her a tight-lipped smile. "What about you, Alexis? You must know how to dance, seeing as your name was listed as captain." An eyebrow wormed its way up.

I wanted to say, "Well, my sister is a cheerleader, and she's taught me a thing or two," but that would be stretching the truth. The main thing Kate has taught me is to bug off! Instead I said, "I'm captain because the dance group is my idea. See you tomorrow." My heart pounded as I walked away, leaving Olivia and Bianca with their mouths gaping open.

Once I was back next to Mom, I unhooked my bag from her shoulder and asked her for the keys so I could wait in the car.

"I'm ready," Mom said. "I've got milk in the back of the van that needs to be put in the refrigerator."

Not before I made myself the biggest glass of chocolate milk to celebrate. Who knew I could stand up for myself in front of Bianca and Olivia! Thank You, God.

Love, Lexi ♡

Dear Lexi,
Do not be afraid and do not panic. For I will personally
go ahead of you. I will neither fail you nor abandon
you. (Deuteronomy 31:6)
Love, God

God Is Your Helper

What are you afraid of? Are there people or situations that intimidate you? Being afraid creates doubt—in yourself and in what God is doing in your life. Fear not only stops you from doing things you are capable of but also makes you forget about God. When you are afraid or intimidated, take a deep breath and pray. God is your helper and will always be there for you.

What's YOUR Story?

Dear God,

I'm afraid. Here's why:

_____

_____

_____

_____

_____

_____

_____

_____

_____

_____

But when I remember that you are my helper, I feel . . .

_____

_____

_____

_____

_____

_____

_____

_____

_____

_____

_____

_____

_____

_____

_____

Thank you for always being there for me. Help me to
pray when I am afraid!

Love, _____

> *The LORD is my helper,*
> *so I will have no fear.*
> *What can mere people do to me?*
> Hebrews 13:6

Friday, September 16

Dear God,

All last night I thought about what Justin had said about making Bianca a cocaptain of the dance team. Part of me wanted to ask her, but a bigger part of me just couldn't do it.

Abby pulled me aside before tryouts and told me the things Bianca had been saying in the quad during lunch:

"Who does Alexis think she is?"

"I'm the best dancer. I should be captain."

"I might not even try out. That'll show her!"

As much as Bianca's words hurt, I wouldn't let them distract me from my decision. I was in charge of that dance team!

If there was going to be a dance team. So far, it was just Ellie and me.

My armpits were sticky as I waited for Bianca and the Honey Bees to enter the gym. I glanced at Mrs. Dykstra, sitting on the bleachers grading papers. At least I had a witness in case Bianca showed up and it got ugly.

A few girls walked in, none I knew very well.

"Is this where the dance tryouts are?" a dark-haired girl asked. I thought her name was Sydney. Or was it Sarah?

"Yes." I smiled and pointed to a clipboard that had my crinkled sign-up sheet attached to it. "This will be the order of tryouts. If you haven't signed up already, you can do it now."

The girls pushed each other forward, obviously none of them wanting to go first.

I glanced at my watch. Tryouts were supposed to start in two minutes. Where were Bianca and the Honey Bees? They were first on the list.

"I hope Bianca doesn't show up," Ellie whispered. "These girls seem nice."

"They may be nice, but that doesn't make them good dancers," I whispered back. "We really need Bianca."

"Well, it doesn't look like Bianca or the Honey Bees are coming." Ellie looked like she was holding back a smile. "We should start without them."

Mrs. Dykstra looked up from the stack of papers she was grading, glanced at her watch, then walked over to the sound system and turned on the music.

My toes tapped to the steady beat. "Okay. Ellie, you're first."

"No, she's not. I am!" Bianca strutted in wearing a brightly colored dance costume. The Honey Bees, in the same outfit but in a rainbow of colors, marched in behind her. "Okay, girls. Let's show them how it's done." Bianca struck a pose.

Olivia, Sophia, and Isabella surrounded Bianca and froze in position.

Mrs. Dykstra changed the music to a new song, and the girls started to dance. I've watched enough dance shows on TV to know these girls were good. I hate to admit I was mesmerized. Each move was perfect and in sync. With every second that passed, I wanted to run out of the gym and pretend that I had never tried to be the captain of a dance team.

"Umm, Lexi." Ellie's voice was a bit shaky. "Sydney and her friends just left."

The routine ended.

"Thank you, Bianca, Olivia, Sophia, and Isabella. I'll post the list of people who made the dance team on the school bulletin board on Monday." Did those words just come out of my mouth? I sounded more confident than I felt.

Bianca's eyes narrowed. "What about Ellie? Doesn't she have to try out?"

"Of course," I said, "but—"

"But the dance group needs six members, and there's no one else here. That must mean we all made the team." Olivia smiled.

Even I could do that math. I grabbed the clipboard. "Like I said, I'll post the list Monday."

"Fine." Bianca huffed and stormed out, with the Honey Bees close on her heels.

Mrs. Dykstra turned off the music, collected her things, and waved at Ellie and me before heading out the door.

Ellie and I stood there staring at each other.

"Looks like we're on a dance team with Bianca." My voice sounded too cheery for the situation.

Ellie's face scrunched up like she'd bitten into a lemon. "You mean YOU'RE on a dance team with Bianca."

"C'mon, Ellie. We're in this together." I clutched the clipboard to my chest.

"You saw them. There's no way we can learn a dance like that in two weeks."

"What if I promised you Kate will help us? Would you change your mind?"

Ellie, being the oldest, has always wanted an older sister and thinks my sister can do no wrong. Ha! I doubt Kate will give Ellie or me the time of day. But I wasn't going to burst Ellie's bubble, not when the possibility of reaching popular status was within reach.

"You think Kate would do that for us?" Ellie's face softened, hope in her eyes.

"My mom already told her she had to. It's a done deal!" I beamed.

Ellie giggled. "I can't believe what you said to Bianca and the Honey Bees. You've got guts."

I couldn't believe what I'd said either. But as I replayed the words in my head, I realized Justin might be right. If this dance group had any chance of succeeding, Bianca should be cocaptain.

An hour later I lay on my bed, coloring.

"Don't tell me you're making another sign." Kate dropped a pile of textbooks on her bed.

Instead of stating the obvious, I changed the subject. "Got a lot of homework this weekend?"

"What gave you that idea?"

I could've said the same thing a moment ago to Kate, but unlike my sister, sarcasm isn't my first language. But I gave it a try. "Oh, I don't know. Maybe because you brought a pile of books home . . . and you look so happy."

"Very funny." Kate rolled her eyes.

Something wasn't right. As sarcastic as Kate was, she didn't seem herself.

"Got boy troubles?" I ventured. She NEVER shares secrets with me, but maybe tonight was different. If only she'd open up and trust me! Maybe then we could actually have a close relationship.

"What? No. All the boys like me, remember?"

Yeah, right! I know she has her eye on a boy a year older, but Mom and Dad have told her she can't date until two months from now, when she turns sixteen.

"Girl troubles?"

"Lexi, let it go. All right?"

So I wasn't the only one with an enemy. Maybe Kate wasn't as popular as I thought. I filled in the last few bubble letters announcing the list of dance team members.

Kate changed into her cheerleading uniform to get ready for tonight's football game.

I tried not to look, but it was nearly impossible as I listened to Kate wrestle with the zipper on the side of her skirt.

"Can I help?" I asked.

"No, you can't! There's nothing you can do."

Serves me right for trying to be a caring sister. I turned away and concentrated on putting the markers back in the box.

"Okay, fine," Kate said. "But promise me you won't tell Mom and Dad."

That was a loaded statement. How could I promise

something when I didn't know what I was agreeing to? "Why? What did you do?"

"Nothing **that** bad. It's just that Mom and Dad paid so much money for my cheerleading uniform. After today I might not get to wear it for a while—if ever."

"But the school year just started—"

"Thanks for the reminder." Kate jammed her feet into her shoes and tied the laces.

"Why won't you get to cheer?" I asked.

"Never mind. You're not old enough to understand." Kate grabbed her megaphone and slammed the door on the way out.

Maybe it was better that she didn't tell me. Now I don't have to keep anything from Mom and Dad. God, I'm glad YOU know everything! Growing up is so complicated.

Love, Lexi

Dear Lexi,
I created all the stars and call each one by name.
Because of My power and strength, not a single one is
missing. (Isaiah 40:26)
Love, God

God Knows Everything

Nothing is hidden from God's sight. The Bible tells us He knows our thoughts, when we sit down and when we stand up, and what we're going to say before we say it. In fact, God knows us better than we know ourselves. You can trust God with what's going on in your life and in other people's lives, because He has it all figured out. God knows everything!

What's YOUR Story?

Dear God,

Someone is keeping a secret from me! Here's what's happening:

_____

_____

_____

_____

_____

_____

But I can trust that you know everything, because . . .

91

_____

_____

_____

_____

_____

_____

_____

_____

_____

_____

_____

_____

_____

Thank you for knowing everything about me and other people. Help me to trust you!

Love, _____

How great is our Lord! His power is absolute!
His understanding is beyond comprehension!
Psalm 147:5

Saturday, September 17

Hi, God,

Today was the first day in WEEKS that I got to hang out with Abby at her house. We cut pictures from magazines, painted our fingernails, and listened to music.

Abby clicked on a new song as I practiced my dance moves. "You're not that bad. At least you have rhythm."

"But choreographing a song is next to impossible. I know, I'll snap my fingers while Bianca and the Honey Bees dance around me. Won't that look awesome?" I rolled my eyes.

"You forgot Ellie. What will she do?"

I shrugged my shoulders. "I don't know. Maybe we'll stand together and snap on different beats." I made a silly face and demonstrated.

"Didn't I tell you it was a crazy idea?" Abby laughed. "Why did you start a dance group anyway?"

I'd been asking myself the same question all day, and then remembered the goal of this whole operation. "How is hanging out in the quad?"

Footsteps on the stairs halted our conversation. "Abby?" Her mom's voice drifted down the hall.

"What's up?" Abby asked when she appeared in the doorway.

Abby's mom held up three tickets. "How would you girls like to go to a concert at Living Faith Community Church tonight?"

Abby and I clung to each other and jumped up and down

like we'd just won the lottery. "We're going to a concert! We're going to a concert! We're going to a concert!"

Her mom laughed. "Wouldn't you like to know who's playing?"

We stopped bouncing.

"Oh, no!" Abby grimaced. "Don't tell me it's old people music."

Her mom shook her head. "What would you do if I told you it was Way Arrow?"

Abby and I looked at each other and totally FREAKED OUT!

Way Arrow is only the best new contemporary Christian boy band around! (Ha ha, but I guess you already knew that, right?)

I was sure my grounding from the computer wouldn't stop me from going to a church to see a concert. Mom wouldn't be that cruel, would she?

"I'll need to ask—"

"Lexi, I've already called your mom, and she said you can go."

Abby and I high-fived each other.

Either Mom was super tired because Dad was still gone on his business trip and wanted me out of her hair, or she actually knows I AM IN LOVE WITH WAY ARROW!!! Either way, I was going to see my favorite band in—I glanced at the clock on Abby's nightstand—three hours! "Pinch me," I said to Abby. "Have I died and gone to heaven?"

"Hmm. I have an extra ticket," Abby's mom said. "Who do you think would like the other one?"

"ELLIE!" Abby and I screamed in unison.

The next few hours c-r-a-w-l-e-d by.

We changed outfits at least ten times, and I straight-ened Abby and Ellie's hair. Mine would take too long because it's one BIG frizzy mess. Instead, Ellie let me borrow her sparkly headband, which actually looked pretty cute. Then we practiced what we'd say if we actually got to meet the guys in the band.

"Hi, my name is Alexis, but you can call me Lexi." I smiled into the mirror at my reflection and saw food stuck in my braces. GROSS! Thank goodness I saw it before meeting Way Arrow!

"I'm going to ask for their autographs," Ellie said.

Abby nodded. "Me too."

"Good idea." I remembered the $20 bill my mom put in my wallet for emergencies. This definitely qualified as an emergency! Because I would die from disappointment if I didn't get a signed poster from Way Arrow.

"Maybe we'll get some good ideas for the dance group." Ellie cut into my thoughts.

"Yeah," I agreed, even though I knew I wouldn't become a dance sensation overnight no matter how much music I listened to.

A half hour later, we sat in the middle of the audito-rium waiting for the concert to start. Some people filed in with their whole families, but mostly girls filled the room.

Abby whispered, "Look who got a front-row seat."

I craned my neck to see Bianca and the Honey Bees sitting smack-dab front and center.

"Way Arrow is definitely going to notice them." Ellie frowned.

"Who cares? We're here for the music, right?" I said, even though deep down I knew what Ellie said was true.

Suddenly, the lights dimmed and colored spotlights appeared. One by one, the band members came onstage and started playing the introduction for their first song. Joshua, Daniel, Matthew, James, and Thomas rocked the house for an hour and a half. The speakers shook, the deep bass sound blasting through my head and chest. Throughout the concert, we stood, sang along, and clapped.

When it came time for Way Arrow to sing their last song, Joshua motioned for everyone to sit down. "I'd like to call one audience member up onstage. Who knows all the words to our song 'Home to You'?"

My hand shot up, along with a bunch of other people's throughout the audience, including Bianca's.

"All right." He grinned. "You in the front row. Come up onstage."

Bianca bolted to her feet and dashed up the steps. She stood real close to Joshua and looked up at him as if he were a piece of steak she wanted to devour.

"Ready?" He smiled and started strumming his guitar. The song was slow and soothing, like a lullaby. My favorite line was when they sang about one day meeting Jesus in heaven. Everyone clapped when they were through, and Bianca bowed like she was the star of the show. Joshua gave her a side hug and motioned for her to take a seat.

UGH! Why does Bianca get to experience everything

awesome while I'm stuck in the middle? I crossed my arms over my ungrateful heart and tried to shake the jealous thoughts away.

The house lights came on and the pastor walked across the stage. "If you'd like a Way Arrow CD, poster, or T-shirt, you can purchase them in the lobby immediately afterwards and meet the members of the band. Some of the proceeds from the concert will be given to support orphans and widows in the community. Thank you for coming!"

One nice thing about sitting in the middle was that we were in line to meet Way Arrow before the people sitting up front.

We inched forward, and my heart raced. What if I said something stupid? Would they roll their eyes like Kate does?

"My mom gave me money for a T-shirt," Ellie said.

"I'm buying a CD. What about you, Lexi?" Abby asked.

"Poster. I'm getting a poster," I repeated, my words sounding wobbly and nervous.

I needed to get it together . . . and QUICK! We were next in line.

Ellie and Abby went first. They purchased their items and waited for me to speak.

I took a deep breath. My hands shook as I tried to fish my money out of my wallet. "I'm a big fan."

"Thanks," one of the band members said.

I didn't know which one spoke since my eyes were focused on my wallet, trying to find my emergency money. Where was that $20 bill?

The woman behind me ordered a CD and a T-shirt while I continued to fumble through my wallet. The money wasn't there. Did Kate steal it? Or did Mom need it to buy groceries? Maybe Ben took it? My mind raced through the possibilities.

No matter what had happened, I wasn't going to buy a poster or get Way Arrow's autograph!

"You can always borrow my T-shirt," Ellie said as we made our way to Abby's car.

"Yeah, and you can listen to my CD anytime," Abby added.

God, I'm happy I got to go to the concert, but my eyes stung and I blinked back tears the whole way home.

Love, Lexi ♡

> Dear Lexi,
> I made this day. Rejoice and be glad in it.
> (Psalm 118:24)
> Love, God

Choose JOY!

You can choose to be joyful despite your circumstances. It's okay to feel sad when bad things happen to you, but don't let your sadness settle into bitterness or pessimism.

When you have a relationship with God, you can choose joy because the Holy Spirit lives inside you. God gave you all that you have. Why not thank Him for each and every blessing?

What's YOUR story?

Dear God,

Something bad happened today. Here's what's going on:

_____

_____

_____

_____

_____

_____

_____

_____

_____

_____

_____

_____

_____

I can still choose to be joyful because . . .

_____

_____

_____

_____

_____

_____

_____

_____

_____

_____

_____

_____

_____

_____

Thank you for all my blessings. Help me to be joyful
despite my circumstances.

Love, _____

Always be full of joy in the Lord. I say it again—rejoice!
Philippians 4:4

Sunday, September 18

Dear God,

I'm starting to understand why Mom says you move in mysterious ways!

Here's what happened.

During junior high group at church, a few kids talked about Way Arrow and the stuff they had bought at the concert.

I slunk down in my seat and crossed my arms, mad all over again at the missing emergency money and the fact I didn't get to buy an autographed poster. Ellie must have caught on to how I was feeling, because she covered her new Way Arrow T-shirt with her jacket.

That only made me feel WORSE!

Suddenly I was more determined than ever to figure out where my emergency money had gone.

Once I got home, I raced to my bedroom and started rummaging through Kate's stuff. I checked under her pillow, between the mattress and box spring, and under her bed.

Next, I dumped the contents of her backpack on the floor and flipped through the pages of her books. I was headed to her dresser to look through her drawers when Kate came in.

"What are you doing?" Kate's mouth hung open and her eyes were wild and angry.

"Where is it?" I accused, pulling her top drawer open.

"Lexi, I don't know what you're talking about, but you'd better stop touching my stuff or else I'll—"

"What? Tell Mom?" I threw her socks on the floor. "I know you took it!"

So far I hadn't found the money. I was going to feel EXTREMELY stupid if I was wrong and Kate hadn't stolen it.

"Please, stop." Kate's voice softened.

I shut the drawer and took a breath. I was out of control, but Kate would've done the same thing if she thought I was stealing from her.

"Did you take my money?" I asked.

Kate nodded. "Yes, but I'll return it by the end of the month when you need to turn in your orders."

My orders? "So you stole my emergency money AND the money from my chocolate and cookie dough envelope?" Suddenly I felt sick.

"What? Of course not!" Kate shook her head, a shocked look on her face. "I would never touch your emergency money. How mean do you think I am?"

I hesitated. Did she really want me to answer that question?

"I'm sorry, I should have asked," Kate continued. "I promise I'll give you the ten dollars before next week."

I wanted to know what she needed the money for but decided to let it slide. At this point it didn't matter, and I doubted she'd tell me anyway.

"Well, if you didn't take my emergency money, then where did it go?" I crossed the room and plunked down on my beanbag chair.

Kate gathered the stuff on the floor and shoved it in her backpack. "What's your emergency?"

Why should I tell Kate about the Way Arrow poster when she never confides in me? "Never mind. Forget I mentioned it. It's too late now anyway."

"Whatever." Kate shrugged a shoulder and continued to clean up her stuff.

Suddenly, the truth smacked me in the face. If Kate didn't give me the ten dollars soon, I'd need to come up with it somehow!

"You better pay me back . . . and don't you dare take any more!" I pushed myself up and slammed the door on the way out.

Mom met me in the hall with a basketful of laundry. "What's all the racket?"

Might as well come right out and ask her. "Did you take the emergency money from my wallet?"

"Oh, I forgot to tell you. Ben needed it for a class field trip. I'll replace it as soon as I run to the bank," Mom said. "Say, you never told me about the concert. How was it?"

I didn't get a signed poster from my ALL-TIME FAVORITE BAND because of Ben? I balled my hands into fists.

"It was great," I said through gritted teeth. "Except I wish I could've bought a poster. They were signing them and EVERYTHING. But my money was gone."

"Oh, no! I'm so sorry," Mom said.

The doorbell rang, interrupting our conversation.

"I'll get it!" I raced down the steps and looked through the window.

Mrs. Hollsworth, the woman who was behind me in line after the concert last night, stood outside.

When I opened the door, she handed me a large, rolled-up piece of paper. "Hi, Lexi. I thought you might like this."

Was it what I thought it was? Could it be? I slipped off the rubber bands and unwound it.

Mrs. Hollsworth bought me a Way Arrow poster?

YES, YES, YES!!! I jumped up and down and did a few twirls.

The band members signed it and EVERYTHING!
It said:

To: Lexi

   Keep rockin' for Jesus!

From: Joshua, Daniel, Matthew, James, and Thomas

"Thank you so much!" I felt like hugging Mrs. Hollsworth, but I wasn't sure if that would be weird.

"I wanted to give it to you last night, but I lost you in the crowd," Mrs. Hollsworth said.

"How did you know I wanted a poster?" I hugged it to my chest.

"I heard you tell your friends. Do you like it?"

"Like it? I LOVE IT!" I grinned.

"Good. See you next Sunday in church." She smiled and walked down the street.

Mom came up beside me. "Wasn't that sweet of her?"

I definitely agreed.

Love, Lexi

Dear Lexi,
I cause everything to work together for the good of
those who love Me and are called according to My
purpose for them. (Romans 8:28)
Love, God

His Divine Plan

Bad things happen—sickness, death, and natural disasters, to name a few—but the Bible says that everything works together for good for those who love God. He cares about the smaller stuff in your life too—your struggles in school, drama with your friends, frustration with your family. We don't see the whole picture of what God is doing, but He has a plan. Whatever the circumstance, rely on God's promise to carry you through.

What's YOUR story?

Dear God,

I'm really disappointed. Here's what's happening:

_____

_____

_____

_____

_____

_____

_____

_____

_____

_____

_____

_____

_____

_____

_____

_____

_____

_____

_____

I can give my worries and cares to you by . . .

_____

_____

_____

108

_____

_____

_____

_____

_____

_____

_____

_____

_____

_____

_____

_____

_____

_____

_____

_____

_____

_____

_____

_____

_____

_____

Thank you for caring about the big stuff and the smaller stuff in my life. Help me to rely on you.

Love, _____

Give all your worries and cares to
God, for he cares about you.
1 Peter 5:7

Monday, September 19

Dear God,

I hid in a bathroom stall during break.
   Why?
   Because I had just hung up the sign on the bulletin board announcing the dance team members and I was totally FREAKING OUT!
   There's nothing surprising about the list (Bianca, the Honey Bees, Ellie, and me), except the fact that I wrote Bianca's name as choreographer. But let me make one thing clear. She is NOT in charge! And she can't kick me off my own dance team.
   The door to the girls' bathroom swung open, and I pulled up my legs so no one could see me.
   "They're definitely outnumbered." I recognized Bianca's voice.
   "Maybe the dance will be too hard and they'll quit," Olivia said.
   "I'll make sure it is," Bianca said.
   "We could do the dance that won us the state competition last spring," Isabella added.
   "Perfect!" Bianca and the Honey Bees said in unison, their laughter echoing off the walls.
   I clutched my knees to my chest and held my breath, even though I wanted to burst out of the stall and tell those girls exactly what I thought of them. Of course, I just sat there and did nothing. Why humiliate myself and make the situation worse?

The bell rang, letting everyone know it was time to get to class. When I felt like it was safe, I opened the stall door.

I didn't think anything of it when I heard a toilet flush, but I nearly had a heart attack when Bianca walked out!

Where were Abby and Ellie when I needed them?

"Hi, Alexis. Smart choice, making me choreographer." Bianca washed her hands, then applied lip gloss across her perfectly plump lips.

"I hope so." As I said the words, an idea zipped through my mind. I wanted to do a happy dance right there in front of Bianca, but of course I didn't. Why prove to her I can't dance very well before the first practice?

Instead, I asked, "Can you meet me after school so we can talk about the dance?"

"Talk? How about the girls and I show you what we have in mind?" The lip-glossed smile Bianca sent me gave me the shivers.

I had to regain control of the situation, and FAST!

"Ellie has to babysit today. How about tomorrow?"

"Okay, but there are only eleven days before the school assembly. You and Ellie will need all the practice time you can get." Bianca grabbed her backpack and strutted out of the bathroom, her shiny hair swinging in perfect rhythm with her steps.

What had I gotten myself into?

I didn't tell Ellie or Abby what I'd overheard. They'd warned me the dance team was a crazy idea, but I didn't listen.

When school ended, I dragged myself out the door to the bus and plopped into the first open seat, not caring how far I was from the cool kids in the back.

Ellie sat down beside me. "What's wrong with you?"

The bus was not the time or the place to let her know what was really going on. I straightened in my seat and pushed my lips up into a smile. "What makes you think something is wrong?"

"Lexi, you don't fool me. You've been moping around all day. Who died?"

Not who, but what! Bianca killed my dream of being popular with one overheard conversation.

The boy in front of us swiveled in his seat. "I'm glad you're still captain of the dance team, Lexi. Way to show Bianca she doesn't own middle school."

Ellie nudged me with her elbow and grinned.

"Well, she doesn't." I emphasized each word with a little too much enthusiasm.

It won't take long before everyone in school finds out Bianca really does control everything and everyone—me included.

The kid turned back around, and I let out a sigh.

"We can do this!" Ellie whispered. She had a determined look on her face, something I hadn't seen since I thought up this crazy idea.

I bit my lip. "I'm not so sure."

"At least we won't go down without a fight," Ellie said.

I imagined six cats in a tangled mess with bared teeth and sharp claws. Not pretty!

I shook the thought from my head.

"You're right," I said. "No matter what, we can't give up. We owe it to the rest of the kids at Green Acres Middle School to try! They expect a dance at the assembly, and we're going to give it to them."

I held up my hand and we did our secret handshake, which always puts me in a good mood.

Clap bump clap bump snap bump FLAMES!

Suddenly I actually believed Ellie and I could do the dance!!!

My happiness lasted until I walked into the house. Mom sent me to Ben's room so she could talk with Kate. The pinched look on Mom's face only meant one thing. Kate was in trouble!

Maybe Mom found out Kate took the 10 dollars from my chocolate and cookie dough envelope. Or maybe she discovered the reason Kate said she wouldn't get to cheer.

Either way, Kate was going to blame ME for blabbing.

Except I didn't!

Okay, I might have accidentally said something to Ben, but I didn't think a five-year-old would remember.

Here's what happened.

Last night after I hung up my new Way Arrow poster, I read Ben a bedtime story to help Mom since Dad's still out of town.

When I finished reading, Ben's eyes were closed, and I just started talking. Pretty soon I'd told Ben all about Kate stealing my order money and how she didn't think she was going to cheer after this week.

"Serves her right for being so mean," I said. It was

then that I realized Ben was wide awake! I told him to forget what I said, but as I sat in his room waiting for Mom and Kate to finish talking, the guilt of spilling the beans gnawed at me.

Kate would never trust me again! Not that she ever trusted me in the first place.

"Ben, can I move in with you?" I pushed the pile of toys aside and sat beside him on the floor.

"Sure." He smiled.

The only problem is Ben's room is a lot smaller than mine and there isn't enough space for all my stuff. Plus, it would be awkward to share a room with a boy.

After Ben and I played a game of Chutes and Ladders, Mom peeked her head in the doorway. "Lexi, you can go to your room now."

"Does Kate hate me?" The question popped out before I thought about what I was saying.

"Why would Kate hate you?" Mom asked.

"Oh, I don't know. When does she not hate me?" I laughed it off, attempting to cover my tracks.

Mom handed me a $10 bill. I wasn't sure if it was to replace part of the emergency money or to help Kate repay me for the money she owed. Either way, I appreciated it.

"No one hates anyone," Mom said.

I could argue that point, but why make a bad situation worse?

Kate was sitting at her desk studying when I walked in. I wondered how long it would take for her to start yelling at me, but it never happened. Strange!

An hour later, a folded piece of paper came flying my direction. This is what Kate's note said:

Thanks for NOT telling Mom.
Thanks for telling Ben.
It feels good to tell the truth.
You're still annoying! Ha ha

Maybe I'll never find out why Kate needed money or why she might not get to wear her cheerleading uniform after this week, but I have enough problems of my own.

I grabbed a pen and wrote back:

You're welcome!

I folded the paper and tossed it at Kate, then studied for my history test.

As I write this letter, I'm a bundle of nerves thinking about tomorrow's dance team meeting with Bianca and the Honey Bees. YIKES!

God, please give me strength!

Love, Lexi

Dear Lexi,
Don't get tired of doing what is good. At just the right
time, you will reap a harvest of blessing if you don't
give up. (Galatians 6:9)
Love, God

Don*t Give Up

Did you know perseverance builds character? Giving up is easy, but finishing what you've started takes work. God wants you to stay strong even when you feel like quitting. He has unlimited power and is able to help you deal with anything you are going through. Call on God. He will give you strength.

What*s YOUR story?

Dear God,

I want to give up. Here's what's going on:

_____

_____

_____

_____

_____

_____

_____

_____

_____

_____

_____

But I can finish what I've started by . . .

_____

_____

_____

_____

_____

_____

_____

_____

_____

_____

Thank you for your unlimited power. Help me to stay strong.

Love, _____

I can do everything through Christ,
who gives me strength.
Philippians 4:13

Tuesday, September 20

Hey, God!

Today I woke up with a headache and sore throat.

Mom made me stay home from school because we were waiting on a phone call from the lab to see if Ben had strep throat, and she was afraid I had it too!

I didn't mind lying on the couch watching cartoons and having Mom fix me hot tea and toast. Plus, I had another day to study for my history test.

But around 1:00 p.m. my brain kicked into gear, and I realized today was the day Bianca and the Honey Bees were going to show Ellie and me the dance. And now I wasn't going to be there! UGH!

Without me, Ellie was sure to walk out and quit the team! Somehow I had to convince Mom to drive me to school.

That's when I had the brilliant idea of picking up my homework! I was sure Mom would take me to school so that I wouldn't get too far behind. Right?

WRONG!

Mom said not to worry, and that if I rested and didn't get a fever, I could go to school tomorrow.

If I didn't show up for that dance meeting, Bianca might think I was quitting the team, and I couldn't let her gain the upper hand!

I had to get to school to defend myself. But HOW?

As another episode of Ben's favorite superhero cartoon

flashed across the television screen, I strategized how I could sneak out of the house and catch a bus.

After a few minutes thinking about that idea, I realized it would never work. I get lost easily and would probably end up in another state! Besides, I was being kind of devious and had already been grounded from using the computer for a couple more weeks. Why give Mom another reason to be disappointed in me?

Instead, I came right out and asked her. (Thank you, God, for helping me do the right thing! I'm really trying to listen to YOU!)

At first Mom didn't think it was a good idea because of Ben's possible strep throat. But then she remembered she had to pick up medicine at the pharmacy and could drop me off on the way as long as I didn't have a fever.

Thank goodness my temperature was normal!

I still wasn't feeling that great, but there was no way I was going to miss dance practice.

When I got to school, I went to the office with a note from Mom excusing my absence, then searched for Ellie, all the while trying to ignore my scratchy throat.

"There you are," I said, spying Ellie in the gym locker room.

"Where have you been?" Ellie hugged me so tight I thought I was going to barf.

I freed myself from her grasp. "Miss me?"

Ellie sighed. "You have no idea!"

"C'mon." I smiled and tugged on her arm. "Let's go see the dance!"

Bianca and the Honey Bees walked into the gym.

Obviously Bianca didn't think I was going to show up today, judging by the disappointed look on her face.

While Ellie and I watched them perform, my head started pounding and I felt like I was going to throw up for real. Had they been practicing all weekend?

I told Ellie to close her mouth, which was hanging wide open in DISBELIEF and SHOCK. Yeah, they were that good!

At that moment I wished I'd stayed home in my pajamas, watching television and snuggling under my favorite fuzzy blanket, where it was safe.

Then I remembered the reason I wanted to be captain of the dance team in the first place—to hang out in the quad with all the popular kids. And even if I never become popular, I want to learn the dance and do my absolute BEST!

Besides, sometimes you just have to get out of your comfort zone and try something new!

"Ready to learn the dance?" Bianca lifted an eyebrow, her question more like a challenge.

"You bet we are. Right, Ellie?" I glanced at my best friend, hoping she remembered our secret handshake.

"Um, yeah, sure." Ellie didn't sound very convincing.

For the next twenty minutes Bianca bossed us around:

"Step left."

"Move right."

"Hop forward."

"Hands up."

"Jump back."

"Kick."

"Double twirl."

I felt dizzy and nauseous. I had no idea if it was from Bianca, the dance, or the fact that I woke up feeling sick this morning. No matter what, I didn't want to give the PD the satisfaction of me quitting on the first day of practice. But I wasn't going to last much longer.

Just then Mrs. Dykstra walked into the gym and stopped the music. "Lexi, your mom is waiting for you outside. She said you stayed home today with a sore throat. You really should go."

"What?" Bianca had a horrified look on her face. "You're sick? EWWW! Get away from me. I'd better not get sick because of you." She flipped her hair over her shoulder, grabbed her backpack, and strutted out of the gym.

The Honey Bees glared at me and followed after Bianca.

I wanted to shout, "THANK YOU, MRS. DYKSTRA! YOU'RE THE BEST!" But of course, I kept quiet.

Ellie and I looked at each other and started giggling.

One day of practice down—ten to go.

God, please help us survive!

Love, Lexi

> *Dear Lexi,*
> *Patient endurance is what you need now, so that you*
> *will continue to do My will. Then you will receive all*
> *that I have promised. (Hebrews 10:36)*
> *Love, God*

Stick with It

You need to practice a skill for a long time before you master it. The Bible describes patient endurance as calling on God's power to give you strength (Isaiah 40:28-31). If you have this kind of endurance, you will finish what you begin. So have faith and stick with the good things you start, even when they get tough. When you endure, you show trust in God.

What's YOUR Story?

Dear God,

I need endurance. Here's why:

_____

_____

_____

_____

_____

_____

_____

_____

_____

_____

_____

_____

_____

_____

_____

_____

_____

_____

_____

_____

I can show patience by . . .

_____

_____

_____

124

_____

_____

_____

_____

_____

_____

_____

_____

_____

_____

_____

_____

_____

_____

_____

_____

_____

_____

Thank you for giving me the strength to finish what I begin. Help me to depend on Your power.

Love, _____

*We also pray that you will be strengthened with all
his glorious power so you will have all the endurance
and patience you need. May you be filled with joy.*
Colossians 1:11

Wednesday, September 21

Dear God,

Thank goodness Ben and I don't have strep!

Turns out it's seasonal allergies. Mom gave me some medicine, and I feel normal again—as normal as I can be. (Some people, like Bianca, may argue that I'm NEVER normal.)

Anyway, as much as I like staying home and watching television with my little brother, it felt good to climb out of bed and get ready for school.

Except Kate is in a BAD MOOD! It's hard to tiptoe around someone when even normal things, like closing dresser drawers a little too loudly, send her over the edge.

Here's what I know:

Last night when Dad finally came home from his business trip, I overheard him and Kate talking.

Okay, I was actually spying, but I had to find out why she stole my order money and the reason why she might not get to cheer.

Turns out she paid someone to do her homework and was caught cheating on a test! YIKES!

I didn't stick around to find out what Dad thought about the whole situation. Instead I snuck back to my room, jumped under the covers, and pretended to be asleep.

When Kate came into the room, I thought I heard her crying. As hard as it was, I kept quiet. The last thing Kate needed was a nosy little sister asking her questions. But now she's a grouch with a capital G, and I can't get out of our room fast enough!

I wish I had a room of my own.

Maybe I could move into one of Abby's spare bedrooms, at least until she moves to New York. Mom, Dad, and Ben might miss me, but Kate definitely wouldn't! It's hard being a middle child. As much as I try, I can't make everyone happy.

I was still mulling this over when I arrived at school.

Ellie rushed up to me the minute I entered the building. "Did you hear the news?"

My mind twirled in all kinds of directions. "What news?"

"Bianca is having a sleepover this Friday night, and we're invited!"

"Really?" My voice squeaked.

"Yes! Look what I found in our locker." Ellie whipped a piece of paper from her backpack.

The invitation said:

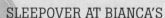

SLEEPOVER AT BIANCA'S
When: Friday, September 23, at 6 p.m.
Bring: Sleeping bag, clothes, makeup, cell phone
Why: Girl time!

I shook my head. "I never thought in a MILLION years that the most popular girl in middle school would invite us to a sleepover!"

"Right?" Ellie smiled.

We jumped up and down and did the secret handshake. Clap bump clap bump snap bump FLAMES!

Abby approached. "What's all the excitement about?"

Ellie shoved the invitation into her backpack. But Abby has been my friend as long as Ellie has, and I didn't want to keep secrets, so I came right out and told her the news.

"You guys aren't going, right?" Abby looked from me to Ellie and back again. "She's the meanest girl in seventh grade."

"We're on the dance team together. If we don't go, Bianca might get mad." It sounded logical to me, but the confused look on Abby's face meant she didn't agree.

"What's going on with you two?" Abby asked. "You've never cared about popularity until this year."

"Hey, don't judge your best friends," Ellie said. "We're just trying to get into the quad like you."

"Well, if you haven't noticed, you are still my best friends, and I'd rather hang out with both of you."

"But if Ellie and I got into the popular crowd, you wouldn't have to choose," I said.

"It's an easy choice." Abby crossed her arms and narrowed her eyes. "We've been friends for years."

I had to think of something FAST!

"The sleepover is really no big deal," I said. "After the dance is over, I doubt Bianca will give us the time of day."

"Yeah," Ellie said. "In ten days she won't even know we exist."

The truth is, Bianca isn't the only one I'm trying to impress. I want everyone to like me! Going to a sleepover at Bianca's house equals popularity by association.

"Well, I hope you guys aren't making a big mistake." Abby shook her head and walked off.

Were we? Ellie and I stared at each other.

During the day I didn't have time to think about the sleepover because I had to make up the history test. Mr. Kramer ran out of copies and arranged to have another student give me the test orally since the copy machine in the office was broken. We were supposed to meet in the library during sixth period.

My mouth dropped open when I saw Justin Powell walk in!

I couldn't believe I was going to have my crush all to myself for the next forty-five minutes. Then again, if I didn't know any of the answers to the test, I would flunk and Justin would think I was a complete idiot.

My hands started to sweat, and my heart beat a funny rhythm.

Boom-BOOM, boom-a-boom-BOOM.

Then again, maybe Justin was at the library to check out a book . . .

He sat down beside me. "Ready for your test?"

"I'm not sure," I answered honestly.

Justin smiled. "You'll do fine."

I whipped out a piece of paper, trying to stop my hands from shaking. I felt pretty good as the test went along. There were a couple of questions that stumped me, but overall it wasn't that hard.

When the test was over, Justin put the teacher's copy in a folder, along with my answers, and tucked them inside his backpack to give to Mr. Kramer. "Easy, huh?"

"Yeah. It wasn't too bad."

A few seconds went by with Justin and me just staring at each other, waiting for the other person to speak. Talk about AWKWARD!

I looked away first.

"I saw you made Bianca choreographer of the dance team." By the tone of Justin's voice, he obviously approved.

"Yeah." I nodded. "But after watching the dance, I'm not sure it was a smart idea."

"Why?" Justin asked.

I wondered if I should tell him about the conversation I'd overheard in the bathroom about how Bianca and the Honey Bees wanted Ellie and me to quit, but I didn't. Instead I said, "The dance is hard!"

"That's never stopped you before." He flashed me yet another grin.

Does Justin have to be so . . . ADORABLE?

At that moment I wondered what it would be like to be his girlfriend, but then I remembered the note Ellie gave him a few weeks back and how he wrote that he liked me as a friend. I tried not to let that thought dampen my mood.

"Thanks for the vote of confidence," I said, "but I'm not sure Ellie and I can pull it off."

"If it's too hard, let Bianca know. Remember, you're the captain of the dance team and have the final say."

RIGHT! I'd forgotten about that. "But first, we want to give it our best shot! You know, pride and all."

All during dance practice I kept reminding myself of my conversation with Justin, especially when I had to relearn the moves from the day before, when my head was spinning and my throat felt like it was on fire.

"No, Lexi, you go left, not right."

"We raise our arms and spin like this."

"Why can't you and Ellie remember what to do?"

Like Mom says, Rome wasn't built in a day, and Ellie and I won't become amazing dancers overnight. It takes practice. Lots and lots of practice!

Unfortunately, we only have nine days until our dance performance and two days until the sleepover, when Bianca and the Honey Bees expect us to know the routine.

Suddenly I thought of the perfect solution.

I asked Ellie if I could borrow her cell phone so I could record the moves. That way Ellie could e-mail it to me and we could learn the steps at night when we're not at school.

"Good idea," Bianca said. "But wait. You don't have a cell phone?"

I'd been hoping she wouldn't notice.

"Not at the moment," I said, "but I'm going to get one soon." How soon is anyone's guess, especially since I spend all my money on chocolate.

"I hope you have a cell phone by my sleepover. You are

coming, aren't you?" Bianca studied her cuticles like she didn't care one way or the other if I'd be there.

"I don't see a reason not to." I shrugged a shoulder, acting as nonchalant as I could.

"By that time you'll know the dance. Right?"

"Right."

Then reality hit! I'm grounded from the computer for the rest of the month. How am I going to download the dance now?

I'm such a loser.

Love, Lexi

Dear Lexi,
Even before I made the world, I loved you and chose you in Christ to be holy and without fault in My eyes. (Ephesians 1:4)
Love, God

Holy and without Fault

God loves you even when you make mistakes. Before you were born, God knew you were going to sin, and yet He chose to love you, blemishes and all. If you have accepted Jesus as your Savior, God sees you as holy and without fault. So, ask for forgiveness and learn from your mistakes, rely on God's power, and believe He loves you.

What's YOUR Story?

Dear God,

A bad choice is coming back to haunt me. Here's what's happening:

_____

_____

_____

_____

_____

_____

_____

_____

_____

_____

_____

_____

_____

I know You see me as holy and blameless because . . .

_____

_____

_____

134

_____

_____

_____

_____

_____

_____

_____

_____

_____

_____

Thank you for loving me even when I make mistakes. Help me to seek forgiveness and believe you chose me— blemishes and all.

Love, _____

Now [God] has reconciled you to himself through the death of Christ in his physical body. As a result, he has brought you into his own presence, and you are holy and blameless as you stand before him without a single fault.
Colossians 1:22

Thursday, September 22

Dear God,

There was no dance practice today. Bianca said it's a waste of time until Ellie and I learn all the steps.

Fine by me!

Little did Bianca know I practiced for an hour last night. Kate downloaded the video for me so that I wouldn't get in trouble with Mom and Dad for using the computer. Yes, I promised to make Kate's bed for a week, but it was so worth it. She even helped me learn the dance. Can you believe she was being nice for a change?

Anyway, back to today.

I took my time walking home from the school bus, kicking rocks and glancing up every so often at the puffy clouds in the sky. It felt good to have a few minutes to myself.

When I got home, the CUTEST little tan-and-white kitty was sitting on my front porch! As I petted the top of his head, I noticed his sparkly blue collar. I had a strange feeling I'd seen him before. He purred loudly and followed me into the house.

Okay, I actually let him in because I desperately wanted to keep him. Except the second he rubbed up against Mom's leg, she started to sneeze.

"Where did that cat come from?" Mom grabbed a tissue and blew her nose. "My allergies! Please, get him out of here."

I picked him up, brought him into the garage, and

settled him on a pile of dirty laundry next to the washing machine. He purred as I stroked his back. Guess we weren't going to have a pet even though I've wanted a cat since I was SIX!

My mind took a turn. What was a nice cat doing on my doorstep? He must have an owner somewhere.

Something wasn't right.

I flipped the laundry basket on top of the cat so he wouldn't escape, then ran outside and retraced my steps back to the bus stop. There it was!

The sign said:

MISSING
Tan-and-White Cat
"Snickers"
Very friendly
$100 Reward
Please call: 555-4559

I had glanced at the sign on my way home from school. No wonder the cat looked so familiar.

I ripped the sign off the telephone pole and raced back to my house, dreaming of the cell phone I was going to buy with the reward money, just in time for Bianca's sleepover.

"Mom, look!" I showed her the piece of paper. "Do you think it's the same cat?"

"Why don't you call the number and ask?" Mom handed me the phone.

I don't know why I get so nervous talking to people, but my hands get clammy and my mouth dries up. Basically, I never know what to say.

"I've got this." I gave myself a pep talk as I took the phone to the garage to call and see if the person could identify the cat I found—or I should say, found me.

Personally, I wouldn't want to give away a perfectly good cat if it wasn't to the rightful owner. Maybe I could keep him in my room, or Mom could take allergy shots or something. You never know. It just might work.

But once I started talking to the woman on the other end of the line, my hopes of keeping the cat were dashed. He was definitely Snickers.

The woman told me her name was Mabel and mentioned the sparkly blue collar and said his new name tag came in the mail today. She'd be happy to show it to me if I could bring her the cat. Apparently she lives in the retirement community two blocks over.

Then she asked me if I'd ever seen a $100 bill!!!

When I told her I hadn't, she laughed a sweet, grandma type of laugh and gave me her address.

I wondered if Mabel liked chocolate and cookie dough. I made sure the packet and order form were in my bag, just in case, then went back to the garage to get the cat.

Except the dirty pile of laundry was gone. So was Snickers! The washing machine whirled and hummed, and I imagined a very wet cat in the spin cycle. I didn't know whether or not to open the washing machine, but I was going to have a heart attack if I did nothing.

Meow

"MOM!" I yelled at the top of my lungs.

As I waited for her to come into the garage, I searched the shelves and in between the lawn mower and bikes. No Snickers!

How was I going to tell Mabel that I'd lost her cat all over again? Not to mention that the $100 reward was slipping through my fingers . . .

Just when I felt like giving up, I noticed something move inside the car. It had to be Snickers, right? Unless it was a raccoon . . . or a SKUNK! The window was open, and I cautiously peered inside.

"Meow!" Snickers swished his tail.

Phew! "There you are!"

I opened the car door and picked up the cat before he bolted. "Come here, you. Time to take you home to Mabel." And collect my reward.

Mom made Kate walk with me to Mabel's house to drop off the cat. On the way there, Kate hounded me about the reward money.

"You're going to take money from a sweet old lady for a cat who showed up on our doorstep? Seems selfish to me." Kate smacked her gum.

"Hey, I'm the one who remembered the missing cat sign. If it weren't for me, Snickers wouldn't be going home."

"Then you should give me some of the money for walking you there."

Was Kate serious? A minute ago she thought I was selfish!

I decided to ignore Kate the rest of the way. Why have a conversation with her when everything she said made me want to scream? Of course I resisted the urge. Why get in trouble and risk the sleepover?

When we got to Mabel's house, she opened the door right away and took the cat from me. "There's my baby! You've been on quite the adventure, haven't you?" Mabel nuzzled her face against the cat's neck. "Thank you so much for bringing him home. Give me a minute and I'll be back with your reward."

As Kate and I waited by the front door, I started feeling guilty. Maybe Kate was right and I shouldn't take money for a cat that just appeared at my house. Then again, it was Mabel's idea to offer a reward. Besides, a new cell phone was on the line—and so was my reputation with Bianca and the Honey Bees.

As I flip-flopped back and forth, Mabel reappeared at the door with the cash in hand. "Here you go. One hundred dollars, as promised."

I hesitated.

"Please take it, dear. If it weren't for you, Snickers would still be lost or back at the shelter."

That sounded logical to me! As I took the money, I imagined the new cell phone and cool case I would buy. Suddenly I couldn't wait for Bianca's sleepover.

Before Mabel closed the door, I whipped out the catalog for chocolate and cookie dough and told her how the school was raising money for a new computer lab.

That's when I found out Mabel is diabetic and can't eat sugar, but she was happy to take the catalog to bingo tonight with all her friends at the retirement center.

PERFECT!

I can't wait to see how many orders I'll get. I bet enough to win the limo ride and pizza lunch!

The whole way home I couldn't wipe the smile from my face, even when Kate told me how goofy I looked.

Love, Lexi

Dear Lexi,

I will take care of you and supply all you need from My glorious riches, which have been given to you in Christ Jesus. (Philippians 4:19)

Love, God

All You Need

There is a big difference between needs and wants. God promises to give you all you need, not all you want. Basic food, water, and shelter are examples of *needs*; going out to a movie, buying designer clothes, and having the newest form of technology are *wants*. (Get a babysitting job, sell clothes you've outgrown, or do extra chores around the house to earn money for the wants on your list.) Are you facing a situation where you don't know how your needs will be met? It can be really scary when one of your parents loses a job or your family faces an unexpected expense. When that happens, don't forget to pray. Ask God to show you how He's going to provide, and be prepared to be amazed!

What's YOUR Story?

Dear God,

I need You to answer my prayer in a BIG way. Here's what's happening:

_____

_____

_____

_____

_____

_____

_____

_____

_____

_____

_____

_____

_____

_____

_____

But I know you will take care of me and give me all I need, because . . .

_____

_____

_____

_____

_____

_____

_____

_____

_____

_____

_____

Thank you for supplying all I need. Help me to appreciate everything you have given me.

Love, _____

All glory to God, who is able, through his
mighty power at work within us, to accomplish
infinitely more than we might ask or think.
Ephesians 3:20

Hi, God,

I'm hiding in my sleeping bag with a flashlight to write this letter.

Here's why.

Mom worked later than usual, and I had to wait for Dad to take me to Bianca's house for the sleepover.

My knees shook as I waited for Bianca to answer the door. I prayed Ellie was already there, but then I remembered she wasn't coming until after she finished babysitting.

When Bianca opened the door, I wanted to race back to the car and go home.

What was I thinking, accepting an invitation from a girl who hates my guts? She's been nothing but mean to me since last year. Besides, I wasn't able to buy a cell phone. Mom and Dad said they'd discuss my chances AFTER I'm done with being grounded for using the computer. I glanced one more time at Dad's car as he drove away.

Too late to go home now!

Bianca led me to the kitchen. "We're eating pizza and drinking root beer. We would've waited for you, but I didn't think you were coming. You're an hour late!"

"Yeah, about that," I said, dropping my sleeping bag and backpack in the corner. "I would've come sooner—"

"Doesn't matter." Bianca cut me off.

I glanced around the room, suddenly wanting an adult

around. I was swimming in shark-infested waters, and I felt like the bait. "Where are your parents?"

Bianca opened the pizza box and grabbed a slice. "Away for their anniversary. My Aunt Kathy is upstairs, but she promised me she'd leave us alone unless we ABSOLUTELY needed her."

I filed that thought in my brain. It was nice to know I had a potential ally. After snatching a piece of pepperoni pizza, I joined Olivia, Sophia, and Isabella outside, sitting around a table.

"Where's Ellie?" Bianca asked.

The Honey Bees barely noticed me, only glancing up when I said Ellie would be coming around 8:00 p.m.

Olivia leaned over and whispered to Bianca, loud enough for me to hear. "Should we tell her now or later?"

Bianca sent Olivia a wait-until-later signal, then directed her gaze at me. She pointed to a metal tub filled with ice and soda on the far end of the patio. "Want a root beer?"

I had a feeling Bianca wanted me out of earshot, but I wasn't going to budge, even though I was thirsty. "Maybe later."

"Did you learn the dance?" Isabella asked, her mouth full of pizza.

I nodded. "My sister helped me. She's a cheerleader." I don't know why I felt the need to remind them of that fact. It wasn't as if Kate was going to give me instant popularity.

"Did Ellie practice with you?" Olivia eyed Bianca.

I bit into my pizza and a slice of pepperoni fell,

sticking to my shirt. Perfect! Now I'd have a red stain for the rest of the night, reminding me what a loser I am. I pulled off the pepperoni, nabbed a napkin, and swiped at the remaining sauce.

Bianca laughed. "Well, did Ellie practice with you?"

"No, she didn't," I said, suddenly feeling like I was a criminal on trial, and Bianca and the Honey Bees were the judge and jury. I zipped up my sweatshirt to hide the stain. "But I'm sure she practiced at home."

"I hope so," Olivia said. "She needs all the help she can get."

"Look what I baked." Bianca shifted everyone's attention to the dessert sitting on the kitchen counter.

It hurt to hear Bianca and Olivia talk about my friend. I wanted to defend Ellie, but the PD and the Honey Bees had already scrambled to the kitchen to stuff their faces with brownies.

I followed behind, carrying a can of root beer. Suddenly I had a flashback of Bianca pouring soda over my head in the quad. I wondered what Bianca or Olivia would do if I dumped soda over one of them. The thought made me smile. As tempting as that was, of course I did nothing. The night had just started, and I wasn't about to jeopardize the dance team.

So I joined in and ate a brownie. WOW! They were AMAZING! Even if the night turned out to be a total flop, the brownies were worth every minute I had to spend with Bianca and the Honey Bees. Yes, I LOVE chocolate that much!!!

In fact, I even got up the nerve to ask Bianca for the recipe.

She raised a brow and folded her arms across her chest. "I'm not telling. It's a secret."

The secret is her mom probably made them.

I had to think of another way to pull the recipe out of Bianca. "So what did you do? Add a whole bag of chocolate chips?" I took another brownie and bit into it. YUM!

"If you really want to know, ask Justin. He knows my secret." Bianca tried to act coy, but she knows I like Justin, and she wanted to rile me up.

"How would he know?" I muttered under my breath, and then wanted to kick myself for falling into her trap.

Bianca giggled. "Because I gave him a brownie today and whispered my grandma's secret ingredient in his ear."

The doorbell rang, stopping me from saying something I shouldn't.

Thank goodness Ellie was here! At least now I had a true friend here, instead of only girls who would gladly stab me in the back.

"Ellie, so glad you came." Olivia's voice dripped with sweetness. "Now we can practice, right, Bianca?"

"First let Ellie put her stuff down and have a brownie, unless Lexi ate them all." Bianca looked my direction and smirked.

I let the jab roll off my back. After all, I live with a mean older sister and hear things like that on a regular basis.

LOVE ♥ CHOCOLATE

Maybe if I gave Bianca a compliment, she'd be nice the rest of the night. Yeah, right!

But I had to try. "Hey, what can I say? I love chocolate, and you make really good brownies."

Ellie set her things next to mine and sent me a what-have-we-gotten-ourselves-into look.

Isabella turned on the dance music. "Hurry up, let's practice."

I thought I did okay keeping up with Bianca and the Honey Bees, but Ellie fell behind and went the wrong direction a few times, aggravating the PD. Honestly, I wish everyone had to learn a new dance instead of only Ellie and me. The pressure is EXCRUCIATING!!!

After a half hour, Bianca called it quits. She rolled her eyes and reminded Ellie and me that we agreed to be ready by tonight. If I hadn't started this dance group, I would've walked out and never looked back. Those girls were vultures, and I wouldn't have been surprised if Ellie quit on the spot.

That's when I came up with the BEST possible solution!

"Why don't Ellie and I practice while the rest of you do something fun, like hair and makeup? Give us twenty minutes—"

"Or thirty," Ellie chimed in.

Bianca and the Honey Bees huffed and walked off, leaving Ellie and me downstairs alone.

I went over the dance moves like Kate did with me, but by the end of the thirty minutes, Ellie still didn't know the entire dance.

"I need a break," Ellie said. She snuck into the kitchen for a brownie. "These are good!"

"Apparently, Bianca has a secret ingredient, but that's beside the point. C'mon, Ellie. Let's practice."

After some more time passed and no one came downstairs, Ellie and I decided to see what was going on. We held on to each other as we climbed the stairs and called out to Bianca.

Laughter floated down the hall. Were Bianca and the Honey Bees playing a trick on us?

I leaned my ear against one of the closed doors. The sounds of a television and a person snoring echoed through the walls. Must be Aunt Kathy. Some chaperone! I motioned to Ellie to keep walking.

We came to the last door at the end of the hallway and knocked. "Bianca? Are you in there?"

More laughter. I tugged on the door handle. It was locked.

"Let's go back downstairs," Ellie said.

When we turned to leave, the door swung open. Sophia motioned us inside, then locked the door behind us.

"What are you guys doing?" I said, trying to act cool, calm, and collected.

"Come over here and find out," Bianca said.

Bianca and the Honey Bees were sitting in a circle, each on their cell phones. A mound of candy lay in the center and a heap of empty wrappers littered the space.

"Looks like fun! Can I join?" Ellie wiggled between

Sophia and Isabella, whipping her cell phone out of her back pocket.

Without a cell phone, suddenly I was the one who felt out of place. Ellie patted the space beside her. "C'mon, Lexi."

It wasn't long before we discovered Bianca and the Honey Bees were sending hurtful text messages to kids in our class, like this one:

I thought giraffes had long necks, until I saw yours!

As funny as that sounded, the text was MEAN, and I didn't want any part of it.

I breathed a sigh of relief, knowing I wouldn't be asked to join, because I DON'T HAVE A CELL PHONE! I never thought I'd be so happy about that.

Suddenly, Ellie clutched her stomach and said, "What's in those brownies? I think I'm going to be sick." She ran to the bathroom and wouldn't come out until her parents came to pick her up. Personally, I think Ellie felt fine, but she wanted to get away from the PD and go home where it was safe. I don't blame her. I wanted to go home too, but as captain of the dance team, I knew I HAD to stay.

A half hour later, Ellie was gone and I was once again on my own.

The only good thing is that Bianca admitted to putting a special type of chocolate (from Belgium, I think) in the brownie batter, giving away her secret ingredient.

When we laid out our sleeping bags in the family room,

Bianca set hers next to mine. Once the lights were out and everyone was ready for bed, the PD called out my name and whispered something I had expected to hear all night. "Ellie doesn't know the dance, and she'll ruin it for the rest of us unless you convince her to quit the dance team."

Is she right?

Love, Lexi 🤍

Dear Lexi,
Don't be afraid, for I am with you. Don't be discouraged, for I am your God. I will strengthen you and help you. I will hold you up with My victorious right hand.
(Isaiah 41:10)
Love, God

God Is with You

Nothing that happens in your life is a surprise to God. He is with you at all times, everywhere you go, ready to help you. You can endure any trial with God by your side. He fights your battles for you and will pick you up when you are down.

What's YOUR Story?

Dear God,

I'm in a difficult situation and don't know what to do.
Here's what's happening:

_____

_____

_____

_____

_____

_____

_____

_____

_____

_____

_____

_____

_____

_____

_____

_____

_____

_____

152

I know you are with me because . . .

_____

_____

_____

_____

_____

_____

_____

_____

_____

_____

_____

_____

_____

_____

_____

_____

_____

_____

_____

_____

_____

_____

_____

Thank you for always being by my side. Help me to endure when life gets tough.

Love, _____

He renews my strength.
He guides me along right paths,
bringing honor to his name.
Psalm 23:3

Saturday, September 24

Dear God,

I ran out of Bianca's house the minute Mom pulled into the driveway!

What can I say? I needed a break from the PD, the Honey Bees, and anything to do with the dance.

Except after the bomb Bianca dropped on me last night, I promised myself I'd help Ellie before school on Monday, even if it killed me! There was no way I was going to kick her off the dance team.

How am I going to survive practice all week? One night hanging out with Bianca and the Honey Bees was TORTURE.

On the way home, Mom and I stopped by Mabel's house to pick up the order sheet. She sold six tubs of cookie dough and four boxes of chocolate to her friends at the retirement center. YAY, MABEL!!!

While Mabel went to get the money, I played with Snickers and was reminded how much I want a cat. It got me thinking about the SPCA and wondering if they needed someone like me to play with the cats and dogs a few hours a week.

On the way home, I told Mom my plan. She thought it was a good idea since I wasn't allowed to have a pet at home because of her allergies. I couldn't believe my ears!

Even though I was COMPLETELY exhausted from the sleepover, I called the SPCA the second I got home.

When the lady said I needed to be sixteen years old to volunteer, I wanted to scream, "NOOOOO!!!"

I can't even pretend to be sixteen since most people think I look like a ten-year-old. I can't help it if I'm shorter than most kids my age.

I bet people guess Bianca is sixteen. She's as tall as my sister and has a body to match. God, why can't I look more grown-up like Bianca?

Before I hung up the phone, the SPCA lady told me they were hosting a fund-raiser today and to stop by for cookies and lemonade.

At least the whole day wasn't ruined.

As soon as we arrived at the SPCA, we could hear the dogs barking in the background.

I smiled at Ben, who had tagged along.

"Lexi, sorry the volunteer thing didn't work out," Dad said. "But you'll be sixteen before you know it."

Really? I don't think so. Four more years seems like FOREVER! I was about to say something about that when Dad said, "Now remember, we're not bringing a pet home today."

If there is anyone who could convince Dad to adopt an animal, it's Ben. As the baby of the family, he usually gets his way. Being the middle child, I can ask for something for MONTHS and still get no answer.

An older woman greeted us at the door. "Dogs are down the hall to the right, and cats to the left. Please don't feed the cookies to the animals, and enjoy your visit."

Ben tugged Dad toward the dogs, but I wanted to see

the kittens. Dad let me go by myself, saying he'd meet me in the lobby in a half hour.

I snagged a chocolate chip cookie and bolted through the side door. Rows of cages lined the walls. Many of the cats were asleep, but several played with the toys dangling from their cages.

I spotted a litter of kittens in what looked like a playpen on the floor. They were tan and white like Mabel's cat, Snickers.

Honestly, I wanted to hide a kitten in my sweatshirt and take it home, but that would be stealing and would get me in a TON of trouble. Besides, even if I got the cat home, Mom would start sneezing. I kept my hands in my sweatshirt pockets so I wouldn't be tempted.

"Hey, Lexi." I recognized Justin's voice.

I smiled. "Are you here for the cookies?" Did I really ask him that?

"No, my dad's dropping off a sample of his new cat food."

"Your dad makes cat food?"

"Dog food too. Have you heard of Nature Chow?"

I nodded. "The organic pet food? I've seen the commercials on TV."

"Funny you should mention that, because my dad's going to make a commercial for the new cat food. He's going to audition people for the part."

"Why don't you try out for the commercial?" I asked.

"Dad says it's a conflict of interest."

I didn't know what that meant but didn't ask, not wanting to sound stupid.

"I love cats." I smiled. "But I'm sure your dad's looking for an adult . . . or at least someone sixteen." My shoulders slouched. Nothing fun EVER happens to kids my age.

"Auditions are Monday, but if you want to meet my dad, he's here somewhere." Justin glanced around.

It would be SO COOL to be in a commercial. I might even become FAMOUS and become more popular than Bianca!

Life would be PERFECT.

Except I doubted Justin's dad wanted someone with freckles, braces, and wild frizzy hair.

But I had to try. "I'd definitely like to meet your dad."

Five minutes later, we found Mr. Powell unloading bags of Nature Chow cat food in the back room. Justin made the introductions. I smiled real big and told him how much I love animals, especially cats.

"Lexi would be perfect for the cat food commercial," Justin said to his dad while keeping his eyes on me.

I wanted to kiss Justin on the cheek for believing in me, then suddenly the thought of kissing Justin freaked me out. Yikes!

Mr. Powell studied my face. "You know, she does have a nice quality about her." He pulled out a business card from his shirt pocket. "Come by our headquarters Monday afternoon and read for the part."

YIPPEE! I wanted to do a cartwheel right then and there, but I stopped myself, wanting to appear professional and mature. Ha! Who am I kidding? I still have a lot of growing up to do. I jumped up and down a little and slipped Mr. Powell's business card into my jeans pocket.

"There you are," Dad said, his voice stern. Lines crinkled his forehead. "I've been looking for you."

Heat climbed up my neck. Did Dad have to reprimand me in front of Mr. Powell and my crush? That was a good way to lose the part in the commercial before I even had a chance to read for the audition.

"See you Monday." I waved and walked away.

I wanted to tell Dad about the commercial, but I thought it would be better if I waited until he wasn't mad at me for not meeting him in the lobby when I was supposed to.

Ben grabbed my hand on the way to the car. "Dad said we can buy a goldfish at the pet store on the way home."

What did I tell you? Ben always gets his way.

On the drive home, I suddenly remembered I have dance practice on Monday, the same day as the audition!

God, how am I going to be in two places at once?

This is one BIG decision I don't want to make.

Love, Lexi

Dear Lexi,
Trust in Me with all your heart; do not depend on your own understanding. Seek My will in all you do, and I will show you which path to take. (Proverbs 3:5-6)
Love, God

God Will Guide

Are you afraid of making a wrong decision? Figuring out what to do can be very stressful. Many times there are two good options, and picking either one would be fine. Other times, the answer is clear, but we ignore it so we can take the easy way out. Ask God to show you what to do, and let Him be your guide. Remember that He can speak to you through His Word and also through others. Get advice from wise, godly people. Above all, ask God to help you examine your motives and give you the desire to follow His will. It's much easier to follow God's guidance when your heart matches His.

What's YOUR story?

Dear God,

I'm facing a big decision. Here's what's going on:

_____

_____

_____

_____

_____

_____

_____

_____

_____

_____

_____

_____

_____

_____

I ask you to guide me in . . .

_____

_____

_____

_____

_____

_____

_____

_____

_____

_____

_____

_____

_____

_____

_____

_____

_____

_____

_____

Thank you for showing me which path to take. Help me to always seek your will.

Love, _____

We can make our plans,
but the LORD determines our steps.
Proverbs 16:9

Meow

CHOCOLATE

Hi, God,

I waited until after church to tell Mom and Dad about the possibility of being in the commercial for Nature Chow pet food. At first Mom didn't like the idea, but after talking with Dad, she changed her mind and said I could audition!

YIPPEE!

Basically, I think Mom feels bad about the whole cat allergy thing.

I still have to figure out how I'm going to go to dance practice AND the audition . . .

As I was mulling this over, Ellie came over to my house to practice the dance.

Please, Lord, help her remember the steps!

Every time Ellie goofed up, I repeated Bianca's words in my head, "Ellie will ruin it for the rest of us unless you convince her to quit the dance team."

The more Ellie struggled, the more I pushed. "C'mon, Ellie. It's two steps to the left, then kick, and twirl. We've got to get this right if we want to hang out in the quad."

"I'm trying my best." Ellie dropped down on my bed. "Maybe I should quit—"

"NO!" I said a little too harshly, panic rising in my throat. "Remember, on the bus we gave each other the secret handshake and promised we wouldn't quit."

"Yeah, but that was before we saw the dance," Ellie said.

163

I plopped down next to Ellie, held out my hand, and said the chant, "No matter what, we can't give up."

"But it's too hard for me." Was Ellie going to cry?

As sad as I was for Ellie, I felt sorrier for myself when I thought about dancing with Bianca and the Honey Bees without my best friend. I wasn't going to let that happen!

"You'll get it," I said. "We'll practice all day—"

"I have to babysit at three o'clock."

"That gives us thirty more minutes. Please try." I held out my hand again, and after a minute Ellie joined in the secret handshake.

Clap bump clap bump snap bump FLAMES!

As pumped as we were, by the time Ellie's mom picked her up to babysit, she was no closer to remembering the entire dance.

SIGH!

But I told her not to worry, because I'm the captain of the dance team and can change the dance if I want.

Except now that I know the dance, I like it and don't want to change a thing. I'm not as good as Bianca and the Honey Bees, not by a long shot, but at least I remember all the moves.

Ellie, on the other hand, has a long way to go, and there are only FIVE days until the performance.

YIKES!

But I didn't have time to dwell on the dance any longer because I had to figure out how I wanted to look for the audition.

I peered inside my closet and realized I had NOTHING

to wear. Okay, I did have boring school clothes, but nothing that said, "She's the perfect person for the Nature Chow pet food commercial."

That's when I remembered the cute-and-totally-cool jacket Kate bought at the trendy and amazing new store at the mall. She wouldn't mind if I borrowed it, right? I snagged it out of our closet and tucked it inside my backpack. Then I spied the colorful blouse to go with it. I grabbed it off the hanger and stuffed it in my backpack on top of the jacket. Jeans would tone down the look in case I was too dressed up. If I wore that outfit, Justin's dad was sure to pick me.

Of course there was the ENORMOUS problem of my frizzy hair and freckles.

I pulled Kate's magazines off the shelf and flipped through the pages, trying to find the perfect solution.

BAM! Ten minutes later I discovered a couple of easy homemade recipes that were sure to work.

I went down to the kitchen and combined one cup of coconut milk and the juice of a lemon in a glass jar, then tucked it in the refrigerator.

While I waited for the creamy layer to form on top, I cleaned my room. Won't Mom be proud?

Oh, and guess what I found under my bed? A love note to Justin. I'm so destroying it before anyone reads it.

Anyway, once my concoction was ready, I massaged the mixture into my hair and scalp. After 10 minutes, I put a shower cap on my head and wrapped a warm, moist towel around it. After 30 minutes passed, I hopped in the shower and washed and conditioned my hair.

165

WOW, what a L-O-N-G process, but so worth it, because the comb slithered right through the strands!

After my hair air-dried, I looked at my reflection in the mirror and almost didn't recognize myself! My hair looked AMAZING. It wasn't totally straight, but at least it wasn't a frizzy mess.

Next, I followed the directions to get rid of freckles for those with sensitive skin, like me.

I slathered sour cream on my face and let it dry. After a few minutes I wiped it off with a soft towel. I still saw freckles, but they were less noticeable. As I was putting a layer of moisturizer on my face, Kate walked in, and suddenly my day took a turn for the WORSE.

"It's not like you're trying out for Miss USA." Kate scowled at me. "It's a cat food commercial!"

I twirled, showing off my new hair. "You never know— one commercial may lead to hundreds."

"I doubt that." Kate smirked, then pointed to her magazines on the floor. "What's this?"

"I would've googled stuff, but I'm not allowed on the computer, remember?" I picked up the magazines and placed them back on the shelf. Out of the corner of my eye, I saw one of the blouse sleeves sticking out of my backpack. I had to divert Kate's attention. NOW!

Too late.

Kate marched over to my backpack and pulled out her blouse. "And what's this?" Her mouth hung open.

"I was going to ask you—"

"No, you weren't. You were going to steal it!"

"Borrow, just for the audition."

Kate shoved her blouse into her side of the closet. "All you have to do is ask."

Yeah, right! Kate NEVER lets me borrow anything.

Did I dare tell her about the jacket? "If I do ask to borrow something, promise me you won't automatically say no."

"You did lose my favorite lip gloss—"

"When I was eight!" When was she going to let that one go?

"We're totally different sizes," Kate said. "Nothing I have would fit you anyway."

Instead of arguing, I waited until Kate went to sleep before returning the jacket to her side of the closet. I didn't feel right taking it, even if it was only for one day.

Now what am I going to wear to the Nature Chow audition?

Love, Lexi

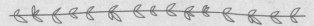

Dear Lexi,
Don't be concerned about the outward beauty of fancy hairstyles, expensive jewelry, or beautiful clothes. You should clothe yourself instead with the beauty that comes from within, the unfading beauty of a gentle and quiet spirit, which is so precious to Me. (1 Peter 3:3-4)
Love, God

168

Beauty from Within

The world we live in, including television, magazines, and movies, sends mixed messages about what makes someone beautiful. But according to God, inner beauty is more important than outward appearance. It's better to focus on being gentle and kind than having perfect hair or flawless skin. The next time you look in the mirror, ask God to help you be the kind of girl who shines for Jesus.

What's YOUR Story?

Dear God,

I'm unhappy about my outward appearance. Here's why:

_____

_____

_____

_____

_____

_____

_____

_____

_____

_____

_____

_____

_____

_____

_____

_____

_____

_____

_____

I can focus on my inner beauty by . . .

_____

_____

_____

_____

_____

_____

_____

_____

170

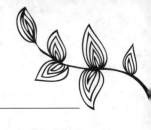

_____

_____

_____

_____

_____

Thank you for creating me—inside and out. Help me to shine for Jesus.

Love, _____

Charm is deceptive, and beauty does not last;
*but a woman who fears the L*ORD
will be greatly praised.
Proverbs 31:30

Monday, September 26

Hi, God,

Kate was right! (Ugh, I hate to admit that.)

NOTHING in her closet fits me. I know, because I tried on shirts, sweaters, and her cute-and-totally-cool jacket. Everything is WAY too big.

"What did you expect? I'm six inches taller," Kate said.

I hate being short!!!

I was about to TOTALLY freak out, when Kate rummaged through my closet and picked out my long cat T-shirt, gray leggings, and pink Converse shoes for the audition.

When I tried everything all together, I have to admit I looked pretty good. Kate gave me the thumbs-up sign, but I don't know if she really meant it or if she just wanted me out of the room.

I guess it doesn't matter. If I'm picked for the part in the cat commercial, they'll tell me what to wear or provide an outfit. Right?

But I knew I wouldn't even be considered for the part if I didn't figure out a way to get to the audition during dance practice!

That's when an idea hit me, and I needed Ellie's help. There was NO WAY I was going to pull this off unless everything went as planned.

Once school was over, Ellie and I met Bianca and the Honey Bees in the gym. I was prepared to give the speech I'd practiced during lunch, but Bianca beat me to the punch.

"We have four days until the performance. If we can't do the dance by now, I doubt we will be able to by Friday." Bianca thrust her hands onto her hips and gave us that don't-mess-with-me look.

"You're right," I said. "If all of us can't do the dance, then we need to change it."

"What?" Bianca glared at me. "That's not what we talked about the other night."

I snuck a glance at Ellie. "As captain of the dance team, I say we need to come up with a new routine, one that everyone can do."

"But we only have a few days," Olivia said. "There's no way we can learn a whole routine by then."

She had a point.

"Okay, maybe not a totally different dance," I said, "but a few changes here and there so that it's not so difficult. We're not trying to win a dance competition, just do a fun routine before the chocolate-and-cookie-dough winner is announced."

As nice as that sounded, that isn't the whole reason I organized the dance team. Truth is, I want to impress the students at Green Acres Middle School so that I'll become as popular as Bianca. Or at least more popular than I am now.

"So what you're saying is the dance is too hard for you." Bianca narrowed her eyes, challenging me.

My audition was in 15 minutes. If I didn't leave right then, I'd be late and miss my chance of being the next cat food spokesperson for Nature Chow. Time to

implement my plan. "Let's break into groups of two and brainstorm ideas—"

"Ellie can come with me," Bianca cut in with a sneer. "No offense, but she really needs help, and let's face it, I'm the only one who can give it to her."

OH, NO! I hadn't planned on the PD stealing my partner. Ellie was supposed to sneak out with me to the audition. My mind raced. Would Bianca try to convince Ellie to quit the team?

I didn't have time to worry about that now. I had an audition to go to!

Isabella and Sophia linked arms, forming a group.

Olivia stepped toward me. "I guess I'm stuck with you."

I had to think of something FAST!

"I need to talk with Mrs. Dykstra," I said, stretching the truth. Honestly, I did have to discuss the music for our routine with her, but it could wait until tomorrow. "I'll be back in a few minutes. Why don't you join one of the other two groups until I get back?"

Olivia passed Bianca a mischievous grin and sidestepped next to Ellie.

Ellie pushed up her new glasses and sent me a look that said, "Please don't leave me with these two!"

What could happen in the half hour I'd be gone? Nothing I couldn't undo once I got back. Right?

I scooted out of the gym before I changed my mind and raced the two blocks to the Nature Chow head-quarters. Huffing and puffing, I walked inside the office, all the while looking around for Justin. Had he noticed my straight hair at school? My lighter freckles?

"May I help you?" the secretary asked, sitting behind a desk in the shape of a bone.

I smiled. "Yes, I'm here for the cat food audition. Justin's dad is expecting me." My voice squeaked, making me sound like a kindergartner . . . or a mouse.

"Go down the hall, second door on the left. Good luck."

I don't believe in luck, but I wasn't about to tell that to the secretary when she clearly thought I needed it. "Thanks."

Once I stood outside the door, I hesitated before going in. What kind of friend was I to leave Ellie the way I did? Should I leave and go back to school?

"Hey, Lexi. Glad you made it." Justin came up from behind me, a smile on his face.

"I hope I'm not late," I said, smiling back and running a hand through my almost perfectly straight hair.

"Nope. Right on time. C'mon in." Justin opened the door and I followed him in. Ellie could take care of herself, right?

"Lexi's here," Justin announced, as if I were the only one auditioning for the part.

Mr. Powell handed me a white piece of paper. "I'll give you a minute to look over the script. Read me the lines when you're ready."

As much as I wanted to take my time, I needed to get back to Ellie. My insides shook like the time I read part of **Snow White** in front of the class. Remembering how Mrs. Dykstra said I did a good job gave me the confidence I needed now.

All I had to do was make a good impression on Mr. Powell. It wouldn't hurt to impress Justin, too. I glanced up from the script. He had positioned himself next to his dad, ready to hear me read my lines.

Wow, he's cute!

But I couldn't let Justin's mesmerizing blue eyes, adorable smile, and perfectly sideswept hair distract me from my audition.

Focus, Lexi!

I started reading. Pretty soon, I was caught up in the part of playing the cat eating Nature Chow cat food.

WAIT . . . WHAT?

To be in the Nature Chow commercial, I had to play the part of a cat???

"You're perfect for the part," Mr. Powell said. "Except what happened to your curly hair?"

"I straightened it," I said, wondering what Mr. Powell and Justin thought of my new look.

"No need," Mr. Powell said. "I like it natural."

"Me too," Justin said.

Who knew my curly, frizzy hair would be an asset? Now I wish I hadn't wasted my time making it straight. Come to think of it, no one complimented my hair at school. Not even Ellie or Abby.

As I was considering that, I spotted a tan-and-white cat costume, complete with cat ears, in the corner of the room. I wanted to die on the spot but didn't want Justin to see how FREAKED OUT I was about the idea of dressing up as a cat to be in the commercial.

Maybe Mr. Powell didn't show me the real script, and I was worrying for nothing.

"There are a couple of other people that need to audition," Mr. Powell said, "but we'll get back to you either way by Friday."

FRIDAY . . . the day of

the dance routine!
the announcement for the limousine ride and pizza
    lunch winner!

AND NOW . . .

the actor chosen to be in the cat commercial for
    Nature Chow!

WOW! Could the day be more IMPORTANT?
Just thinking about it made my hands and feet begin to sweat. I thanked Mr. Powell for letting me audition, then scurried out of the building to get back to school . . . and dance practice!

I was happy to see Ellie, although she didn't look thrilled to see me. Will she ever forgive me for leaving her with Bianca and the Honey Bees?

"Where were you?" Bianca asked the minute I entered the gym.

"I had to take care of something, but I'm here now. What did everyone decide?"

"So now it's up to us?" Bianca asked. "I thought you were captain."

"I am." I tried my best to sound confident. "But you're the choreographer."

"Then I say anyone who can't do the routine should quit," Bianca said. "It's too late to change it now. Right, Ellie?"

Ellie gave me a hard stare. Was I ruining our friendship for the sake of popularity? I'd never allow it to come to that. Would I?

"No one is going to quit," I said. "Let's run through the routine a few more times—"

"Sorry, my mom needs me to babysit," Ellie said.

I wished Ellie wasn't the oldest of six kids.

"Now? But we're not done with practice," I said.

The minute Ellie walked out, Bianca rolled her eyes, her meaning clear. She wanted Ellie off the dance team.

Suddenly, I did too.

Love, Lexi 🤍

Dear Lexi,
Don't be selfish; don't try to impress others. Be humble, thinking of others as better than yourself. (Philippians 2:3)
Love, God

Honoring Others

It's okay to want to do great things and achieve success. But you need to think about whether you want to praise God or if you actually want the praise for yourself. As a Christian, you should try to glorify God in all you do, including how you use your talents. Go after the kind of success you can gain without hurting someone else in the process. By thinking of others before yourself, you are demonstrating God's love and following Jesus' example.

What's YOUR story?

Dear God,

I'm facing a choice to put either myself or others first. Here's what's happening:

_____

_____

_____

_____

_____

_____

But if I think of others before myself . . .

_____

_____

_____

_____

_____

_____

_____

_____

_____

_____

_____

_____

Thank you for giving me gifts and talents. Help me to glorify you in all that I do.

Love, _____

Love each other with genuine affection, and
take delight in honoring each other.
Romans 12:10

Dear God,

If I could use one word to describe today, it would be INTENSE!!!

Here's what happened.

Before school I waited for Ellie by our locker until the tardy bell was about to ring, but she never showed up. I figured she had an appointment of some sort and would come to school a little later.

When she didn't show up by break, I wondered if she was sick.

Or maybe she was so mad at me for leaving her with the PD and the Honey Bees that she'd chosen to stay home from school.

Or maybe she didn't want me to be the cat spokesperson for Nature Chow. I was starting to get upset with her for being jealous, when Abby ran up to me.

"Guess what? We're not moving to New York!"

Abby and I hugged each other and jumped up and down until we caught a few students giving us funny looks.

"So you're staying here," I said, making sure I'd heard correctly.

"Yes." Abby nodded. "Dad decided the move would be too hard on the family. He knows how difficult it is to find close friends."

I agreed.

"Where's Ellie?" Abby asked. "I want to tell her the good news."

I shrugged a shoulder and told her about Ellie being MIA. "Maybe it's her way of quitting the dance team." My words tumbled out, exposing my true feelings.

Abby tugged on my arm and pulled me into the girls' restroom, cornering me by the mirrors. "Okay—what's going on?"

Before I realized it, I had told Abby all about what happened yesterday—about leaving Ellie alone with Bianca and the Honey Bees, the audition for Nature Chow, and Bianca's plan to not change the dance routine so that Ellie would quit.

"Bianca's right. She'll ruin it for the rest of us," I said, suddenly feeling like the worst friend in the world. "So I've made a decision. If she comes to school today, I'm letting her know she's off the team."

Abby's mouth dropped open. "Lexi! You can't do that."

"Yes, I can. I'm the captain. Besides, a perfect dance routine will bring me one step closer to the quad!"

The bell rang, forcing us to go our separate ways to class.

The next two hours until lunch d-r-a-g-g-e-d by! I ate lunch by myself on the bottom bleacher next to the basketball court. Kids walked past without even glancing at me as I sat there eating my peanut butter sandwich.

Justin and his buddies were tossing a football nearby. When the ball landed by my feet, I picked it up and threw it back, not really caring if Justin saw me.

Except today he did.

"Hey, Lexi. Where's Ellie?"

"Why does everyone keep asking me that? I'm not

Ellie's watchdog." I tossed the remainder of my lunch in the trash can, wishing I could throw away my sarcastic comment, too.

"Everyone knows she's your best friend," Justin said. "You two are NEVER apart—"

"Well, we are today," I said, softening my voice.

"Want to use my cell phone? You could text her."

The thought of touching Justin's cell phone gave me goose bumps, until I realized I couldn't remember Ellie's number . . . or how to text. UGH! How embarrassing.

"No, that's okay," I said, trying to act as if it were no big deal. "I'm sure she'd be here if she could. Only a few more days before the school assembly."

"That's right," Justin said. "How's dance practice going?"

The last thing I wanted was for Justin to know how much I was struggling with the idea of kicking Ellie off the team. But in order for me to become popular and reach quad status, I needed the dance to be electrifying, jaw-dropping, and absolutely PERFECT!

"Oh, you know," I said, avoiding the subject.

"Bianca still giving you trouble?"

Does Justin have to be so sweet? And caring?

To be honest, I didn't know if Bianca was the reason for my trouble or if I was making trouble of my own. "Let's just say she's not making my life any easier."

Then Justin said, "Remember what I told you. Bianca's insecure."

I still don't understand how Justin came up with that idea. Frankly, I've never seen a more secure person in my life! At least she pretends to be confident. Could it all be an act?

By the end of the school day, Ellie still hadn't shown up!

I was about to make the big announcement that there were now five members of the dance team instead of six, when Abby stopped by the gym and handed me a note, telling me to read it BEFORE dance practice.

Here's what it said:

Dear Lexi,

I can't believe you're going to make Ellie quit the dance team. She's one of your best friends! You've changed, and in my opinion, not in a good way!

Lately, all you care about is being popular. BTW, hanging out in the quad is NO BIG DEAL. It's not worth losing a friend over.

Please don't do anything CRAZY.

Love, Abby

I shoved the note into my pocket. Is it true? Do I only care about popularity?

"Where's Ellie?" Bianca asked, an expectant look on her face, as if she was hoping I'd already told my best friend she wasn't welcome on the dance team anymore.

I shrugged my shoulders, not knowing what to say.

"She must have chickened out," Bianca said. "Why else would she not show up for dance practice? Unless . . ." She directed her gaze at me.

"Ellie must be sick," I said, stopping the PD from further inquisition. "She hasn't been at school all day—"

"I say we practice as if she's not part of the team," Bianca said. "It'll be better without her."

The Honey Bees agreed.

I stood there and said nothing.

Olivia started the music, and everyone got in position.

Right away I missed the starting beat and had to fight to catch up. If I wasn't careful, the PD and the Honey Bees might try to convince ME to quit!

After going over the song a few times, I realized . . .

Without Ellie, I felt as though I didn't belong.

Without Ellie, dance practice wasn't any fun.

Without Ellie, I understood how hard it is to be the worst dancer!

Suddenly I had more empathy for my best friend.

I wanted to scream, "ELLIE, WHERE ARE YOU?????"

Right there and then I decided there was NO WAY I was going to do the dance without her, even if we weren't as good as Bianca and the Honey Bees.

The second I got home, I raced to the phone to call Ellie. It turns out she wasn't sick at all. In fact, the ONLY reason she wasn't at school was because her mom's car died. Something about the battery.

I've been known to do some CRAZY things, but I wasn't going to tell Ellie what Bianca said about the dance team being better without her.

Anyway, I apologized for leaving her alone with Bianca and Olivia yesterday, and Ellie apologized for missing dance practice. Then she promised she'd do her best and said that she was glad we were in this together.

For just a second I thought about asking if she

187

WANTED to quit the team, but then I remembered Abby's note and how I'd felt without her.

After all, why would I want to hang out in the quad without my best friend?

Love, Lexi ♡

Dear Lexi,
Share each other's burdens, and in this way obey the law of Christ. (Galatians 6:2)
Love, God

A Tender Heart

Having sympathy for a friend means you understand and accept his or her feelings. One of the best ways you can share someone's burden is by being a good listener. When you put yourself in that person's shoes, you will know better how to pray for him or her. God made us so that we can have relationships with other people as well as with Him. When your heart is tender toward others, you are showing God's love.

What's YOUR Story?

Dear God,

I'm trying to understand my friend's feelings. Here's what's going on:

_____

_____

_____

_____

_____

_____

_____

_____

_____

_____

_____

_____

_____

_____

_____

_____

_____

_____

_____

189

_____

_____

I can share my friend's burden by . . .

_____

_____

_____

_____

_____

_____

_____

_____

_____

_____

_____

_____

_____

Thank you for the people in my life. Help me to show your love by having a tender heart.

Love, _____

*All of you should be of one mind. Sympathize with
each other. Love each other as brothers and sisters.
Be tenderhearted, and keep a humble attitude.*

1 Peter 3:8

Wednesday, September 28

Dear God,

Guess What?

I got a callback for the Nature Chow commercial!!!
Here's what happened.

Mr. Powell arranged for Justin to walk with me to the
pet food headquarters during lunch so that I could audition again. I brought Ellie along to watch.

For a second I thought maybe Ellie should be in the
commercial since she's wanted to be an actress since
FOREVER. But then I came to my senses. Ellie doesn't
even like cats!

Once we were inside, Justin told me his dad wanted me
to read the script wearing the cat costume.

"Like a dress rehearsal," Justin said, pointing to the
changing room.

As much as I wanted to be in the commercial, the
thought of wearing an itchy costume made me hyperventilate. "Are you sure you don't want to use a REAL
cat?"

Justin laughed. "Dad says the commercial will be more
memorable this way."

That's what I was afraid of!

The way I saw it, the kids at Green Acres Middle
School would either laugh at me or think the cat
costume was cool.

Ellie helped me wiggle into the costume and zip it up.
Next, I was directed to sit in a chair. A woman fluffed

my hair and applied a layer of makeup before setting a headband with cat ears on my head and attaching a nose with whiskers.

"Meow! You look great." Ellie grinned. "Just purr-fect."

I rolled my eyes. "Very funny!" Frankly, I looked like Mabel's cat, Snickers, except a million times bigger.

"Follow me," Justin said, directing us onto the set that looked like a kitchen.

"There you are! Have a seat." Mr. Powell gestured to the island.

I hopped up on the counter next to the kitty bowl filled with Nature Chow cat food.

I hoped Mr. Powell wouldn't really make me eat the stuff!

"Now read the lines, like you did the other day." He smiled and handed me the script.

I took a deep breath and used my best acting voice. "Give us cats what we deserve. Nature Chow cat food is made with real chicken and salmon. And, unlike the big box brands, Nature Chow never uses artificial flavors, corn, soy, or wheat. Nature Chow, purely delicious!" I licked my lips and rubbed my cat nose with a paw.

"Perfecto!" Mr. Powell kissed the tips of his fingers like an Italian cook. "Lexi, you've got the part. Welcome to the Nature Chow family!"

MY DREAMS OF BEING NOTICED WERE FINALLY COMING TRUE!

I jumped down from the counter and twirled my tail to celebrate. "Thank you, Mr. Powell!"

Ellie rushed to my side and hugged me tight. "You're going to be famous!"

I can't believe I thought Ellie was jealous. She's one SUPER DUPER loyal friend. I felt guilty all over again for wanting her off the dance team, even if it was only for a day.

"Congratulations, Lexi," Justin said, grinning at me with his megawatt smile.

I wanted to hug him, too, but stopped myself. I didn't want to be wearing a cat costume for our first real hug. Talk about AWKWARD!

"I'll send your parents the paperwork," Mr. Powell said. "For now, you'd better hurry back to class."

I wanted to march down the street wearing the cat costume to show everyone how proud I was! But, of course, I didn't. Why make a fool of myself and risk Mr. Powell changing his mind? Instead, I went into the dressing room and took off the costume, placing it carefully over a chair. My future celebrity status depended on that furry cat suit.

The rest of the day went by in a blur. All I could think about was how I was going to be on TV, thanks to Justin, the nicest boy in the ENTIRE seventh grade!

All during dance practice I kept thinking about what he'd said about Bianca being insecure, especially when she glared at me every time Ellie made a mistake. Didn't she know Ellie was trying her best?

Afterward, Bianca pulled me aside. "What happened? I thought we came to an agreement."

"If you're talking about Ellie," I said, "the answer is no—"

"Without her, you could be one of us," Bianca said.

I've learned over the years to think before I speak, especially when talking with someone as sneaky as the PD!

"We're a team," I finally said. "ALL of us."

"You're making a BIG mistake." Bianca flipped her hair over her shoulder and strutted out of the gym.

For the first time since I decided to be captain of the dance team, friendship won over popularity. And it felt good.

Love, Lexi

Dear Lexi,
There is no greater love than to lay down one's life for one's friends. (John 15:13)
Love, God

No Greater Love

A true friend cares, encourages, forgives, and prays. Jesus is the best example of true friendship. He loved you so much that He died on the cross to take the punishment for your sins. God asks you to lay down your life for your friends too, but that doesn't mean you have to die for someone, like Jesus did. Instead, you can put aside your own needs to help someone else. Are you a true friend?

What's YOUR Story?

Dear God,

I'm putting my needs aside for a friend. Here's what's happening:

_____

_____

_____

_____

_____

_____

_____

_____

_____

_____

_____

_____

_____

I can love others like you love me by . . .

_____

_____

_____

_____

_____

_____

_____

_____

_____

_____

_____

Thank you for being the best example of true friendship.
Help me to love others the way you love me.

Love, _____

I am giving you a new commandment: Love each other.
Just as I have loved you, you should love each other.
John 13:34

Thursday, September 29

Dear God,

Who invented braces? They're like a torture device for the teeth.

The funny thing is I used to want braces. Can you believe it? Yep, back when I was a little kid and thought braces were cool. Okay, I know braces make your bite better and your teeth straight, but given the choice, I'd wish for perfect teeth WITHOUT all the metal.

Here's what happened today.

Mom picked me up during English class to go to the orthodontist. Ben came along because he was already done with kindergarten for the day.

"I want braces too." Ben stuck a couple of pieces of string cheese across his teeth as we drove to the ortho-dontist's office.

"Oh no you don't!" I said. "At first your mouth hurts for WEEKS, and it's really embarrassing when food gets stuck in them."

Mom has warned me on more than one occasion not to exaggerate, but this time I was telling the COMPLETE truth! I ~~hate~~ dislike my braces A LOT!

"Braces aren't that bad," Mom said. "Think of the beautiful smile you'll have when you're through."

"I still want braces," Ben said, while trying to keep the string cheese on his teeth. With all that saliva, pretty soon the cheese would turn to mush. Gross!

"Look on the bright side," Mom said. "You can get

green bands around your brackets. They'll look great at the school assembly tomorrow."

Cool! I hadn't thought about getting green bands to match Green Acres Middle School. At least when I smile, it'll look like I have school spirit, even if I mess up the dance.

Please, God, don't let me mess up!

I got sticky armpits just thinking about performing the routine. I grabbed the handle above the opened window to let the cool air dry my underarms.

To be honest, this whole dance thing is turning out differently than I'd hoped, but it's okay because I'm learning what it means to be a true friend.

Once we got to Dr. Salivo's office, the receptionist greeted us. Pam always has a big smile on her face. I guess I would too if I had perfectly straight, white teeth instead of a metal mouth.

"Go on back if you need to brush," Pam said.

Mom and Ben took a seat in the waiting area while I dashed off to brush my teeth. I noticed my gums were a little red and puffy because I haven't been flossing as much as I should. It's hard to use those floss threaders between my teeth, especially my molars in back. But I know it's important to keep my mouth healthy, since the assistant reminds me EVERY time I come.

When it was my turn to sit in one of the reclining chairs, the assistant removed the purple bands around my brackets, as well as the wires.

From my position in the chair, I thought Dr. Salivo looked almost right side up with his goatee and bald head.

"What color bands this time?" he asked after replacing the wires.

"Green," I said, going along with Mom's idea. "For Green Acres Middle School. I'm captain of the dance team, and we're performing at the school assembly tomorrow."

I don't know why I felt the need to explain. Maybe because I hardly ever wear green.

"Good choice," Dr. Salivo said, smiling.

The bad thing about getting new wires is that my teeth are sensitive for several days. Mom usually makes me soup and other soft things to eat until my teeth feel back to normal. Hopefully my mouth will be ready to eat pizza (minus the crust) when I win the grand prize for selling the most chocolate and cookie dough! Yes, I still plan on winning the limo ride and pizza lunch.

In fact, I brought along my order form to the orthodontist's office just in case someone wanted to order. But no one did. I wasn't too surprised, since it's the last day before we need to turn everything in.

After the orthodontist visit, my day took a PERPLEXING turn!

During dance practice, Bianca wheeled in a big suitcase.

Ellie leaned toward me and whispered, "What's the suitcase for?"

"I don't know, but I'm sure we'll find out," I whispered back.

Bianca laid the suitcase on the gym floor and opened it up, revealing short, flouncy skirts and sparkly green shirts. "As captain, Lexi should've thought about our outfits, but I guess it's up to me. Lucky for us, my mom owns a dance studio and had these in storage."

How could I forget something so important?

Maybe because I've NEVER been in charge of a dance team!

Before things went from bad to worse, I had to regain control of this practice, and FAST!

As bummed as I was for forgetting about our outfits, my eyes were glued to the SHIMMERY green shirts. I picked up one of the sparkly tops and held it to my chest. "Thank you, Bianca, for bringing us something to wear."

"Actually, there are only four outfits." Bianca sent the Honey Bees a sly grin. "I'm sure you and Ellie will be able to find something—"

"But the dance is tomorrow!" Ellie shrieked.

"It's not my fault," Bianca said. "If you have to blame someone, blame Lexi."

Even on the last day of practice Bianca made it clear she wanted Ellie and me off the team. Without the same outfits, Ellie and I would stick out as the ones who didn't belong.

Just then an idea popped into my head.

"Why don't we ALL go shopping tonight so we have matching outfits?" I asked.

"Good idea," Ellie said.

"Sorry, we can't." Bianca folded her arms and shook her head. "We're taking a dance class, and it starts tonight."

By the confused look on the Honey Bees' faces, I

could tell they had no idea what Bianca was talking about. I bet she made the whole thing up.

My breath came out in short bursts, and I felt like I was going to EXPLODE! But of course, I didn't.

Basically, Ellie and I had two options:

Demand Bianca and the Honey Bees go shopping and skip the fake dance class so we all have the same outfit.

OR

Go shopping with Ellie and buy WAY BETTER totally-awesome-and-super-cute outfits!

Personally, I'd rather hang out with my best friend instead of the PD any day.

"Fine," I said. "Ellie and I will get our own outfits. But you'll have to like whatever we get."

"You'll try to match ours, right?" Olivia asked, sounding rather annoyed.

It wasn't my fault Bianca only brought FOUR. "We'll do our best." I smiled at Ellie.

But my enthusiasm didn't last.

Once practice was over, Ellie pulled me aside and told me she didn't have money to go shopping. Frankly, I don't either. My reward money from Mabel is in a savings account, and Mom and Dad said it can't be touched.

What are we going to do now?

Love, Lexi

Dear Lexi,
Be thankful in all circumstances, for this is My will for
you who belong to Me. (1 Thessalonians 5:18)
Love, God

Be Content

Even on bad days, you can probably list at least ten things
to be thankful for. When you stop focusing on what you
don't have and remember that God is in control, contentment
follows. Be thankful for your life exactly as it is right now. By
having faith and trust in Jesus, you can always be content.

What's YOUR story?

Dear God,

All I can think about is what I don't have. Here's why:

_____

_____

_____

_____

_____

But if I consider everything You have given me . . .

_____

_____

_____

_____

_____

_____

_____

_____

_____

_____

_____

_____

_____

Thank you for my life exactly as it is right now. Help me
to be content in all circumstances.

Love, _____

I have learned how to be content with whatever I have.
Philippians 4:11

Friday, September 30

Dear God,

Today was the BEST DAY EVER!

Here's what happened.

Once Kate heard about Bianca and the suitcase, she suggested I call the high school cheerleading director and ask if we could borrow last year's uniforms. Guess what? There were enough for all SIX of us on the dance team. YIPPEE!

Kate didn't even pull away from me when I gave her a hug.

I loved wearing a cheerleading uniform and being part of a team, even though my stomach twirled and I felt light-headed when the students filed into the gym for the school assembly.

My family sat in the second row of the bleachers marked for parents and siblings. For the first time in a VERY LONG TIME, I didn't feel invisible. Yes, I'm a middle child and usually not the one people notice, but today Kate, Ben, my parents, and the ENTIRE student body at Green Acres Middle School were going to watch me perform.

I called the dance team together for a pep talk before we went out on the floor. "Remember, doing our best is what's most important, even if we mess up."

Bianca rolled her eyes a little, but Ellie and the Honey Bees nodded in agreement. Then, when no one was looking, Ellie and I did our secret handshake.

Clap bump clap bump snap bump FLAMES!

My heart pounded when Principal Taylor started the assembly. "Ladies and gentlemen, boys and girls, I'm happy to introduce our new dance team members: Alexis, Bianca, Ellie, Isabella, Olivia, and Sophia. Please welcome them as they take their positions."

We ran out, found our spots on the gym floor, and froze in place.

When the music started, we stepped left, moved right, hopped forward, put our hands up, jumped back, kicked, and double twirled in perfect unison until the song was over. I have to admit, WE WERE AWESOME! Not one mistake. Even Ellie remembered all the moves. Thank you, God!!!

The crowd went CRAZY, clapping and cheering. I spotted Abby sitting with the volleyball team. She waved and smiled. Ben bounced up and down in his seat, pumping his fists as if he was the proudest brother in the world. Kate kept her cool but looked VERY impressed. Mom and Dad hugged. It was the BEST MOMENT of my entire life!!!

Until . . .

"Thank you, girls. That was great." Principal Taylor continued with the assembly. "Next, I want to announce the winner of the limousine ride and pizza lunch for the most cookie dough and chocolate sales to help us raise money for new computers."

I squeezed Ellie's hand.

Please, God, let it be ME!

"And the winner is . . . Justin Powell!"

Justin jumped up from his spot on the bleachers, a

HUGE smile on his adorable, can-he-be-any-cuter face, and ran toward Principal Taylor.

"Justin, you can choose up to three students to join you. Who will they be?" Principal Taylor held the microphone to Justin's mouth.

I expected him to choose several of his football buddies.

Instead, Justin said, "Dylan, Ryan, and ... Lexi."

WAIT ... WHAT?

Did I hear him correctly? Justin wanted to take ME?

Ellie nudged me with her elbow and wiggled her eyebrows.

Maybe my crush noticed me after all!!!

I still have mushy feelings for Justin, but the truth is, he's been a really great friend, and I wouldn't want that to ever change.

Wow, what a month! I finally realized that true friendship is way more important than popularity. And above all, YOU matter most, God. Please help me to put you first from now on. And thank you for showing me that even if I'm stuck in the middle, you love me no matter what!

Love, Lexi

Dear Lexi,
Seek My Kingdom above all else, and live righteously,
and I will give you everything you need. (Matthew
6:33)
Love, God

Eyes on Jesus

When we seek God first, everything else will be taken care of. When you put other things first, like material stuff, popularity, or achievements, they take the place that rightfully belongs to God, and they become idols. Seeking God and putting Him first is an every day, sometimes every minute, decision. When you keep your eyes on Jesus, you will be one excited girl for God, knowing He loves you and has wonderful things in store for your life.

What's YOUR Story?

Dear God,

I'm learning to put You first in my life. Here's an example:

_____

When I keep my eyes on you . . .

_____

_____

_____

_____

_____

_____

Thank you for having a relationship with me. Help me to
seek your kingdom above all else.

Love, _____

*Let us run with endurance the race God has set
before us. We do this by keeping our eyes on Jesus,
the champion who initiates and perfects our faith.*
Hebrews 12:1-2

Acknowledgements

It took a team to make this book, and I would like to thank the following people:

First, to my loving family: my husband, Douglas, and my four almost-all-the-way-grown kids—Carson, Brittany, Noah, and Grace. You guys rock!

My parents, Roy and Billie Hoffman, for always cheering me on and supporting my dream.

My wonderful friends and prayer warriors: Marcia, Barbara, Laura, Suzy, Michelle, Kelly, Kira Lee, and Sylvia. You're the best!

To the American Christian Fiction Writers, the Christian Authors Network, as well as the many mentors of the Mount Hermon Christian Writers Conference. Thank you!

My critique partners, Sarah Sundin and Karen O'Connor, for all your grammar changes, comments, and smiley faces. This book is better because of you.

My awesome agent, Rachel Kent, for believing in me and encouraging me in this writing journey. You have become such a dear friend.

To Linda Howard, Stephanie Rische, Sarah Rubio, Brittany Bergman, and the rest of the crew at Tyndale House Publishers. I'm grinning from ear to ear at the privilege of working with you!!!

And most importantly, thank you to my Heavenly Father, who shows me each and every day how much He loves me.

About the Author

SHERRY KYLE has written several books for tween girls, along with women's fiction. Her award-winning book for tween girls, **The Christian Girl's Guide to Style**, was awarded the Gold Mom's Choice Award. Her second nonfiction book for girls, **The Girl's Guide to Your Dream Room**, was nominated for the Christian Retailing's Best Awards.

My Thoughts

My Thoughts

_____

_____

_____

_____

_____

_____

_____

_____

_____

_____

_____

_____

_____

_____

_____

_____

_____

_____

_____

_____

_____

MORE GREAT DEVOTIONALS
FOR GIRLS

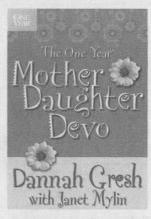

A devo to help moms and daughters connect

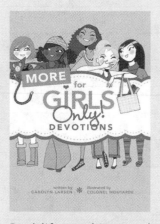

Real-life teachings and illustrations relevant to issues girls face

Do-able daily devos for and about girls

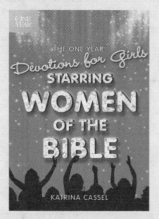

Stories of Bible women for twenty-first century girls

AVAILABLE AT LOCAL CHRISTIAN RETAILERS AND ONLINE.